Emp
Know You...
Irish Law

John Eardly, B.L.

Published in 2008 by
First Law Limited
Merchant's Court,
Merchants Quay,
Dublin 8,
Ireland.

Typeset by Gough Typesetting Services, Dublin.

ISBN 978-1-904480-80-8

A catalogue record for this book
is available from the British Library.

Printed by Lirda

To Marcin Mucha

PREFACE

The reason for this book is to give employees access to information about dealing with problems they experience in the workplace. This is an increasingly important issue as legal rights develop and as the ups and downs of the economy impact on the financial and social well being of employees. However, it also reflects a change of attitude among the workforce in Ireland.

The more I experienced the area of employment law as a practitioner and the more I researched the developing law both in Ireland and other countries, the more I realised that something big was happening in this area of law. This had as much to do with the attitude of people to work as with the introduction of new law protecting employment rights. The court judgments from England and Ireland seemed more to be reflecting a mood rather than simply creating it. This phenomenon was evident in all areas of employment law ranging from discrimination law to personal injury actions and from unfair dismissals to industrial relations. Moreover, organisations as diverse as the Health and Safety Authority, the Equality Tribunal and now the new NERA, as well as trade unions and employer groups, all seemed to be preparing and devising procedures and strategies to accommodate these new developments.

As the author of this book, it seems to me now in 2008 that the information contained here will assist a quite revolution among the workforce. As the author, I am not so much just setting out the legal rights and procedures in a cold, clinical manner but I am also setting out the means to access very important legal rights that affect every worker in the country. There is an increased willingness on the part of workers to do so. While this may relate to the increased confidence of the

Employees: Know Your Rights in Irish Law

Irish workforce that brought about the prosperity of recent years, I also see, in my experience as a practitioner in this area, that many of the rights and procedures to which this book relate to a dismissal or an act of discrimination *after* it has already occurred.

Many employment disputes now arise because workers are not willing to allow a problem to develop in the first place or because there is a perception that the worker is not being afforded the equal treatment or fairness they feel is due to them. In other words, workers are not just simply reacting to changes or decisions in their workplace anymore; they are actively shaping and influencing change and decision-making.

This book gives you access to understanding the system and how you can do this too. The workplace is no longer simply the domain of the boss who hires, fires and promotes his labour as and when required. It seems that employees are, in their own quiet way, taking ownership of the workplace upon themselves and expect it to reflect something of the effort and dignity that they invest in their life's work. This book is an expression of this and I hope will be of much assistance to employees as we go forward into more, rocky economic times.

John Eardly, BL,
October 20, 2008.

TABLE OF CONTENTS

Table of Legislation

CHAPTER 1

Unfair Dismissal Claims

PART A: ARE YOU PROTECTED?

Employees

In order to bring an Unfair Dismissal case to the Rights Commissioner or the Employment Appeals Tribunal, you must be an employee of the person you are suing. An employee includes:

- Anyone working under a **contract of employment**, whether in writing or not.
- For all dismissals occurring from June 29, 2006, **civil servants** (persons employed by or under the State) can bring a claim.
- Anyone who is an **Agency Worker**. If you are an agency worker, you are deemed to be the employee of *the client of the agency* to which you are allocated and not the employee of the Agency itself.

You must be careful in deciding to bring your case to sue the correct party, as otherwise you may risk being out of time and unable to proceed with your case against the person you want to sue.

*For example, if you are bringing an equality dismissal under the Employment Equality Acts 1998-2004 (See Chapter 2 of this Book), agency workers are deemed **employees of the Agency itself** and not the client of the Agency. This is the opposite of the rule under the Unfair Dismissals Acts where* agency workers are deemed the **employee of the client of the agency**. *These are the kinds of things a good lawyer will be able to advise you about.*

Continuity of Service

You must also have at least 52 weeks' continuous service. Notice periods to which you are entitled are included in this period.

Holiday leave entitlements not yet taken are not included in the period to calculate whether you have 52 weeks' service.

For example, where you have served 51 weeks' with your employer and you are entitled to two weeks notice, then if you are dismissed without notice or paid in lieu of notice at the end of the 51st week, you are still deemed to have 53 weeks' service overall as the two weeks' notice are always included even if you are not given them by your employer or you do not work them out.

However, you do not need to show you worked for 52 weeks continuously with your employer where you can show your dismissal is connected with:

    (a) Trade union membership;
    (b) pregnancy;
    (c) breast feeding;
    (d) maternity leave, additional maternity leave or time off for ante or post natal care.
    (e) adoption leave rights;
    (f) parental leave rights; and
    (g) carers' leave rights.

Probation Periods

However, if you are deemed in your written contract of employment to be on probation, then that period of probation does not count towards the service required to bring a case.

An employer is entitled to keep you on probation for a maximum of 12 months.

This is often broken into 2 periods of 6 months each. If after the first six months, the employer wishes to keep you on probation for another six months, he is entitled to do so if this is in your written contract of employment. If you are not kept on after the expiry of the 12 month probationary period, you have no cause of action for an unfair dismissal as you do not have the 52 weeks' service required. Moreover, if you are on 6 months' probation under your written contract of employment and you are taken off probation and made permanent, then that initial 6 month period is not included in the 52 weeks' service required to bring a case.

However, all of this must be put into your contract of employment in writing. An employer cannot impose a probation period on you informally.

Also, if the employer allows the probation period to expire and does not dismiss you or renew the probation period, then that is the end of the probation and you are entitled to be treated as a full employee. He cannot resurrect the probation period after it expires. The employer must abide by the conditions of the probation period in the contract.

Avoiding Liability

Be Aware!
Sometimes, employers may try to prevent their staff from getting rights under the Unfair Dismissals Acts 1977-2001 by dismissing them before they reach the 52 weeks' and then trying to re-employ them later under a new contract of employment.

However, the continuous service of an employee of his employment shall not be broken by the dismissal of the employee by his employer followed by the *immediate re-employment* of the employee.

In previous cases, the Employment Appeals Tribunal has

held that even the issuing of tax forms, i.e. a P45 form, between periods of employment will not be conclusive evidence of a break in continuity. This means that the entirety of the time spent working for the employer will be added up together.

Moreover, if not immediately re-employed but you are dismissed and then re-employed by the same employer *within 26 weeks* from the date of your dismissal, this will also not prevent you from bringing an unfair dismissal claim against that employer.

You must be able to show that the purpose of the original dismissal was wholly or partly to avoid liability under the Act. If you can show this, you can still bring a claim and also rely on the time spent working for that employer under previous contracts so that the overall figure may give you the correct continuity of service with that employer.

Fixed-Term Workers

Fixed-term employees are employees who commence employment knowing that they have only been given a contract for a certain period of time or that their contract is for a specific purpose.

These are to be contrasted with employees who are under a contract of employment of indefinite duration. If fixed-term workers are dismissed as a result of the expiry of the term of their contract, they are not protected when:

(a) The contract is in writing;
(b) it was signed by both parties;
(c) it contains a statement that the Act shall not apply to a dismissal consisting only of the expiry of the term as aforesaid;
(d) this exclusion of protection from the unfair dismissals law does not apply where the fixed term worker enters into a subsequent contract with the same employer for the same

job within three months of the expiry of the earlier contract and if, in the opinion of the RC, EAT or CC, the purpose of the subsequent contract is to avoid liability under the UDA 1977-2001.

Warning!
This means an employer is not allowed to string a series of short fixed-term contracts together in the hope of preventing a fixed term employee reaching 52 weeks' service under one contract.

However, fixed-term workers now also have separate rights under the Protection of Employees (Fixed-Term Work) Act 2003.

Time Limits for Bringing the Claim

You must bring the claim with 6 months of the date of the dismissal or within 12 months if "exceptional circumstances" prevented the making of the claim within the first 6 months. Getting an extension of time to allow you to bring your claim is very difficult, and is normally related to some medical condition of the employee that prevented him or her being able to bring a claim, or some deceit or misrepresentation of the employer as to the reasons for the dismissal.

For example, where you are told your job is redundant and 8 months later you read a newspaper advertisement from your old employer advertising a position very similar to your old job.

This 6 months' limitation does not apply to pregnancy related dismissal.

The date of dismissal runs in the following way:

(a) If the employee is dismissed for ***gross misconduct*** and the employee is sacked

> without working out or being paid his or her
> notice, then the date of the dismissal is the
> date of the termination of employment.

Obviously, one of the claims an employee will make is that no gross misconduct occurred at all in the first place. In this case, the EAT or Rights Commissioner will also award compensation for the lack of notice given by the employer in the event that the employee wins his or her case.

Warning!
However, to be on the safe side, in all gross misconduct cases, it is best to treat the date of dismissal as the date of the decision to dismiss the employee, rather than the date that their notice period would have expired had they been given it.

> (b) If notice is given, the date of dismissal is the
> date of the expiry of the notice.
> (c) If notice is not given and it is **not** alleged
> by your employer to be a gross misconduct
> case, the date of dismissal is the date the
> notice period would have expired depending
> on whether the notice period is statutory or
> contractual which ever is the longer (see
> below). The law provides that everyone is
> entitled to a basic minimum period of notice
> of their dismissal. Your contract may give
> you a longer period. However, your contract
> cannot give you less than the basic period
> provided by the law.
> (d) If payment is given in lieu of notice, the date
> of dismissal is the date on which the notice
> would have expired had it been worked out.

Basic Notice Periods

Period Of Employment	Notice Entitlement
13 weeks to 2 years' service	1 week
2 years to 5 years	2 weeks
5 years to 10 years	4 weeks
10 years to 15 years	6 weeks
Greater than 15 years	8 weeks

Be Aware!
You must also check your contract, as you may have longer notice periods given to you there.

Getting More Than Basic Notice: The Idea of Reasonable Notice

If you have no notice period in the contract or if a court believes that it is too short for the type of work you do, then there is a difference in approach depending on where you take your case. If you are in the Rights Commissioner, EAT or Circuit Court under the Unfair Dismissals Act system, then you will still be given whichever of the above applicable *basic notice periods* apply to you.

However, if you do not take an unfair dismissal claim but take a wrongful dismissal claim to the civil courts (see chapter 3 of this Book), then if your contract of employment does not mention a notice period or if it is too short, the courts will give you *reasonable notice*.

Reasonable notice means that, depending on type of job you do, the courts can give decide to give you the above basic notice entitlements or a much longer period of notice. It depends on what the judge hearing your case thinks is reasonable.

For example, higher professionals such as solicitors, teachers and journalists have been given an entitlement of

*up to 6 months to one year's notice of their termination of
employment.*

Normal Retirement Age

You must not have exceeded the "normal retirement age"
for the employer in question. This means that, where your
employer has a policy of retiring staff compulsorily at a certain
age, then you cannot bring an unfair dismissal case if you are
older than this age when you were dismissed. However, the
employer has to be able to establish that the retirement age is
"normal" for the workplace.

Be Aware!
*In other words, a normal retirement age has to be a policy
that applies uniformly to all comparable staff automatically.
If not, the employer will not be able to establish that there
is a normal retirement age for the workplace and will be
liable for breach of procedural fairness in dismissing the
worker.*

*Police and Soldiers Not Generally Protected Under Unfair
Dismissals System*

Persons employed in the Defence Forces and Garda Síochána
are excluded from bringing an unfair dismissal claim. They
may seek judicial review proceedings of the decision to
dismiss in the High Court.

Be Aware!
**However, members of An Garda Síochána and Prison
Officers can bring a claim under the Equality legislation
to challenge a dismissal or other discrimination (see
Chapter 2). Defence Forces members are also excluded
from equality law.**

Apprentices

Be Aware!
Are you or have you been an apprentice with FÁS?

FÁS trainees under an apprenticeship (not under a contract of employment) are excluded if the dismissal takes place:

- Within 6 months after the commencement of the apprenticeship, or
- within 1 month after the completion of the apprenticeship.

Other Excluded Persons

Officers of Vocational Educational Committees and local authorities are excluded.

Officers of health authorities (except temporary officers) are excluded.

Close relatives of the employer are excluded. This exemption is designed to protect owners of small family businesses and farms.

Fair Dismissals

If the employer has followed fair procedures, the following are fair reasons to dismiss:

(a) Capability, Competence and Qualifications. This means that you are not suitable or performing well enough in the job you were employed to do. However, the decision to dismiss for this reason cannot be made in haste. It must be made after a careful process of warnings and supervision is undertaken.

(b) Conduct. This is when your conduct and behaviour in the workplace makes your

continued employment untenable for the
employer.

(c) Redundancy. This is where, through no fault
of your own, the job, the place of work or the
method of performing the work has changed
so that you are no longer required or suitable
for the role.

Remedies and Financial Loss

If you are successful in your claim, you could potentially be
awarded up to 104 weeks' gross remuneration based on your
financial loss caused by the dismissal.

Be Aware!
However, the phrase "financial loss" is an important one.
This means that you only are entitled to receive what you
can show you lost financially as a result of the dismissal.

Lost remuneration covers not just basic salary but also all
benefits that would have otherwise been received directly
or indirectly whether in the contract in writing or otherwise
arising from the employment. As such, pension entitlements
and bonuses are covered in this loss.

**However, it does not mean that, if you win your case,
that you automatically get 104 weeks' remuneration. It
means that you will be awarded the loss you can prove you
suffered as a result of the dismissal, and that this potential
loss has a ceiling of 104 weeks' remuneration.**

Most employees come out with far less than this ceiling
because their loss is far smaller than 104 weeks' gross
remuneration. This is because many employees are back in
employment and are earning money again within a period of
months after the dismissal. However, certain categories of
workers, such as older employees, may find this harder and
are more likely to be awarded larger compensation awards by

the Rights Commissioner or the EAT (these two bodies are discussed below) to reflect this.

Moreover, the Rights Commissioner and the EAT are entitled to award compensation as is ***just and equitable in all the circumstances of the case***.

This means that, even if you can prove all your losses and win your case, you may still not get all the compensation you are seeking. The Rights Commissioner or the EAT may decide, after hearing the stories of both sides, that you are partly to blame for the events leading up to the dismissal. In other words, you contributed to the dismissal. In order to reflect this, they may reduce the amount of compensation that you are awarded.

Employees who are at risk of this are:

- Those who refuse to cooperate with the procedures of their employer, or
- employees who resign from their workplaces without complaining or giving reasons beforehand to their employer.

The financial loss is based on actual loss and potential future loss of earnings caused by the dismissal. Where no loss has been shown or suffered, up to four weeks' gross remuneration may be awarded.

Social Welfare Benefits

Social welfare payments received on foot of being unemployed (or disability payments where the ill-health is related to the dismissal) are **not** deducted from the compensation awarded to you for the unfair dismissal. This is important as employees on disability benefit and who are certified unfit to return to work are sometimes unable to recover compensation at all because their loss is due to their illness rather than due to the dismissal. In short, if you are sick, the employer will argue that you were not available for work anyway and therefore could not have suffered any loss of salary during this time.

However, in recent years, employees who are able to show that the reason that they are unable to return to work after the dismissal was also the same reason for the dismissal, are entitled to recover loss of earnings into the future while they remain unfit for work. However, it is advisable to be able to show that the disability or illness preventing you returning to work after your dismissal is also connected to the dismissal from your last employment.

Medical Evidence

When your case or compensation is connected to medical issues, as above, you will need to be able to call a doctor or, at least, present a medical report before the Rights Commissioner or Employment Appeals Tribunal or Circuit Court to show this. Normally, you or your legal advisers should seek to get the consent of the employer to submit a medical report of a doctor or consultant to the court. If they do not consent, you may have to arrange to have the doctor there personally to give evidence to the Rights Commissioner or EAT. In this case, you are responsible, as the employee, to discharge their witness expenses for attendance at the hearing.

Reinstatement and Re-engagement

Employees can also look for reinstatement or re-engagement where trust and confidence remains with the employer.

Reinstatement means that the Rights Commissioner or the EAT will order that you be put back into the job you were doing before you were dismissed.

Re-engagement means that the employer is ordered to return you to his or her employment but not necessarily to the same job you were doing prior to being dismissed.

Be Aware!

In both cases, the employer must pay back to you all losses suffered during the period of unemployment and put you into the same position you would have been had you never been dismissed.

Legal Tactics

Sometimes, employees or lawyers seek reinstatement or re-engagement as a strategy to secure a higher settlement out of an employer in the hope that an employer will be so anxious not to have an employee back that they will pay an extra amount of compensation in the hope that they go away.

However, employees and lawyers should know that this strategy can backfire. You must be careful if seeking reinstatement or re-engagement as, on many occasions, the relationship between the parties has broken down so badly it can never be repaired and an employee will not wish to return.

Therefore, if it is sought in the T1-A form, you must be willing to accept it if offered.

If an employer offers reinstatement or re-engagement to an employee in the course of a hearing, this may pull the rug out from under a claimant as s/he may then lose the right to proceed with the claim as the matter has been resolved in accordance with a relief sought by the claimant. Sometimes, an employer uses this tactic as a "double-bluff".

In other words, they know that the employee has no intention of going back and is only threatening this to get a higher settlement. Therefore, by offering reinstatement or re-engagement, they pull the whole rug out of the employee's case.

Under the Counter Payments

Where an employee was in receipt of under the counter

payments, this caused much difficulty in the event that an employee wished to challenge an unfair dismissal.

At law, this traditionally makes the contract an illegal one which the courts will not protect. This makes proceeding by way of wrongful dismissal and injunctive relief (discussed in Chapter 3 of this Book) very hazardous.

However, this is now remedied for an unfair dismissal claim and the employee is entitled to recover compensation in the normal way, and his contract of employment remains valid.

However, the Rights Commissioner or EAT must refer the issue to the Revenue Commissioners. As such, it may be an extra serious threat posed by a dismissed employee to an employer.

Income Tax Allowances

Compensation for loss of earnings is subject to income tax. However, most employees are entitled to a reasonably generous tax free allowance and any award or settlement is subject to Revenue approval: *Taxes Consolidation Act 1997 (as amended)*. Depending on the size of a settlement, tax advice may be sought as to tax efficiency.

PART B: STARTING THE CASE

Now that you know more about when you might have an unfair dismissal claim, if you decide to bring an unfair dismissal case, you have a choice between taking the case either to a body called the Rights Commissioner Service or to a body called the Employment Appeals Tribunal (EAT).

T1-A and T2 Forms

In this area, there are various documents available to you to bring your claim. These documents are available and well explained at the Employment Appeals Tribunal website.

When you bring an unfair dismissal claim, you fill in a document called the T1-A in order to start the case. This is a pre-printed form that is also available from the Employment Appeals Tribunal website. An employer, when he receives a complaint, fills in and returns to the EAT Secretariat a T2 Defence Form (see below).

How Do You Want Your Case Heard?

The decision where you want to take your case must be notified to the Employment Appeals Tribunal when you fill in the T1-A form.

There is a specific section of the T1-A form which asks you whether you object to allowing a Rights Commissioner to hear your claim. You do this by ticking a box indicating whether you object or do not object. If you do not object, then the claim will go for hearing to a Rights Commissioner automatically. If you do tick the box stating that you object, then the claim will be heard automatically by the EAT.

What is the Difference?

The difference between the two relates essentially to the formality and length of the hearing.

A Rights Commissioner, unlike **the EAT**, is a more industrial relations related and a less, formally legal route and will tend to take a practical, more informal and non-legalistic approach to the case. This means that the procedure will feel much less legalistic and more business like.

There will also be much less opportunity to question and ask questions of witnesses brought along either by the employee or the employer before the Rights Commissioner than in the EAT. Also, the hearing is much shorter than a hearing before the Employment Appeals Tribunal.

Written Submissions

If you are going to the Rights Commissioner, normally it is useful to prepare a document called a Written Submission in advance of the hearing for the Rights Commissioner.

This essentially contains the background to what happened to the employee and why the employee says that this is wrong. At least 3 copies of this Written Submission should be made, as a copy must be given to the Rights Commissioner and to the employer or his representative. This can be given to them on the day of the hearing.

The Written Submission does not have to be furnished prior to the day of the hearing.

Dates

The Rights Commissioner hearing is normally finished in approximately two hours. However, there may be exceptional situations where the case may proceed for a longer time. Also, if the case does not finish after the first hearing day, the Rights Commissioner may decide to give the case more time and arrange for a further date when the case will be heard.

Normally, the date allocated will be suitable to both sides, and any dates that do not suit you must be made known to the Rights Commissioner as otherwise you may have to cancel a date allocated to you and this will greatly delay your case.

The Hearing Before the Rights Commissioner

At the hearing itself, the Rights Commissioner will tend to take **a more interventionist approach** and will ask more questions of the parties rather than rely entirely on the solicitor or barrister engaged by the parties.

This does help to speed matters up.

It also helps to level the playing field for those who do not wish to hire a lawyer as the role of lawyers is reduced in the course of the proceedings before the Rights Commissioner since he or she does a lot of the questioning of the parties.

It is often the case that the Rights Commissioner will give time to the parties to see if an out of court settlement or compromise can be reached.

Also, even after the hearing has started, the Rights Commissioner, after hearing some evidence, may suggest an adjournment of the hearing to again allow the parties to reach a settlement.

Employees must be aware that the Rights Commissioner will sometimes be concerned to reach a compromise that he or she believes is practical and reasonable for both sides rather than going through every single detail of evidence that an employee may wish to tell him or her about the case. Settlements are dealt with in this chapter below.

The downside to a Rights Commissioner hearing is that parties, on occasion, feel that they did not get a full opportunity to explain their case or to challenge the defence of the employer. On the other hand, employees appreciate the expertise and expediency with which the Rights Commissioner Service processes its hearings. This is all the more important as employees always pay their own legal costs in this area.

Appeals

If you are unhappy with the determination of a Rights Commissioner, an employee has 6 weeks from the date of the determination to appeal to the Employment Appeals Tribunal.

Be Aware!

There is a specific appeal form called the T1-B. It is a very basic form. All forms needed to bring an unfair dismissal case or an unfair dismissal appeal are on the Employment Appeal Tribunal website.

This appeal is a brand new hearing of the case. However, employees should be careful to **be as consistent as possible,** as any changes in the evidence from the hearing before the Rights Commissioner may be used against the employee by the employer representative in cross-examination before the EAT.

Presenting the Evidence and Questioning Witnesses Before the EAT

If you start off directly at the EAT, it means that you have objected in your T1-A form to the Rights Commissioner hearing your case from the start, then you never go before a Rights Commissioner at all. Instead, you simply wait for a hearing date to be allocated to you by the EAT Secretariat. We will look at this specific procedure below.

If you have been before the Rights Commissioner and are now going to the EAT *by way of appeal*, you will already have been to the Rights Commissioner by now and will have an idea as to what types of issues were raised by the Rights Commissioner. You should try to remember these when you are bringing your appeal as these same issues will most likely interest the EAT also.

You must remember that you must two things before the EAT:

> Firstly, you must be able to explain your version of events to the judges.
>
> Secondly, you must be able to explain why the version of events presented by the employer is wrong. Sometimes, there are facts and events that only the employer will be aware of so you may not be able to deny those directly.

But, it is important to remember that it is not enough to

go into a hearing and tell your story only and ignore what the employer is saying.

The employer will also have his or her story and you must be able to say, as best you can, why this is wrong.

You and your witnesses (if any) must tell your stories to the EAT and ask relevant questions of the employer about his story.

It is very important, if you wish to challenge the employer's version of events, that you put your version of events to him or her first. The reason for this will be explained below. However, questions you may wish to put to your former employer or his or her witnesses are issues like:

    (a) Any contradictions in what they previously said (perhaps before the Rights Commissioner or at a previous hearing day before the EAT).

    (b) Any contradictions between different witnesses for the employer in their version of events.

    (c) Any contradictions between what the employer is saying and any documents that you have. For example, if your employer denies you started in his or her employment at a certain date or that you were made certain promises, you may have letters, emails, payslips. Revenue Commissioner or Social Welfare documents, mobile phone text messages etc from him or her showing he or she is incorrect.

Keep Notes

Always try and keep careful notes or a diary if you are having difficulties with your employment before you are

dismissed, and keep good notes of the evidence before the Rights Commissioner and the EAT during your claim.

If the employer has changed parts of his story at any stage before or after dismissal and between the Rights Commissioner hearing and now, what he or she is saying before the EAT, you are entitled to raise this with the EAT and question the employer as to why he or she has now changed this story.

Also, even if you have not been to the Rights Commissioner, the employer will sometimes change their story even within the course of the one hearing before the EAT. This can happen in the specific ways set out above or in other ways.

If there are differences between the employer's witnesses in what they say, these differences are called "inconsistencies" and you are entitled to ask these witnesses why and how these inconsistencies exist.

For example, one witness for the employer may say that he had a meeting with you on a particular date. Another witness might say that the meeting never took place or took place on a different date. If it is a small difference, the witnesses might just say they made a mistake or they forgot. But if it is a big difference, it is harder for the witness to say he made a mistake.

Therefore, your notes of what is said during the hearing are very useful as the employer will often deny they have changed what they said and you can remind them when you are questioning them in the EAT of what they said either earlier in the hearing before the EAT or previously in the hearing before the Rights Commissioner.

Relevant Information Only

However, you should be careful how you do this. The change of story should be relevant to the case you are making.

Also, it is often enough to raise each change of evidence once.

The EAT judges are very attentive and will often

understand very well the points you are making. They may often stay very quiet and you may be worried that they did not hear the evidence or understand your point. A good EAT judge will often stay quiet as this puts pressure on the witness being questioned to answer a question. If the EAT jumps in, it will often give the witness time to make up another story or will break the train of thought of the witness being questioned. If the judges do not understand your point, they will normally say so. If they do this, it is not to criticise you but simply to ensure that you do not deal with issues that they feel irrelevant in deciding the case.

Be Courteous and Helpful

You would be very wise to remember that you should remain **very courteous and helpful** towards the EAT judges. These three individuals are going to decide your case and you are well advised to be as clear and direct as possible in the way you ask and answer questions.

Obviously, if you have lawyers, they will do this for you and will have experience in spotting contradictions and presenting your story clearly. They will also be able to organise and use any documents that you have that help your case. This is dealt with below.

Representing Yourself

If you are representing yourself, you still have to present your case in the best way possible. You may get some advice during the hearing from the Rights Commissioner or EAT about the issues they want to hear about. However, they must be fair to both sides and remain impartial so you must still be prepared to run your case properly.

You simply go through your story in as orderly and clear a manner as possible. If, in the course of your story, there are documents backing up what you say, you should have those

collected together in one source with page numbers called your
Booklet of Pleadings and be able to point the document out
to the EAT at the same time as going through your story.

If the EAT judges have any questions at any time during
your story, they will ask you directly. Even if you have
lawyers, you must have your documents ready for the case
in front of you open on the table you are sitting at and know
where and on what page to find them at the right time. This is
especially important when you are actually telling your story
to the EAT or Rights Commissioner.

However, you must also be aware of 2 things.

No Scripts Allowed

**Firstly, you are not allowed to read out your story from a
script or make a speech.**

The whole purpose of you telling your story is not only to
set out what happened but also to allow the judges and the
employer to test its accuracy. As such, if you cannot remember
dates or events, this can be a double edge sword as, while no
one has a perfect memory, it may also show that you are unsure
about what you say or about what happened. It is excusable
to forget minor details but you should be aware of the date,
location, time and individuals involved in any major events
in your story. Also, the length of time that has passed since
an event has happened or your age or health may affect the
flexibility given to you by the EAT/Rights Commissioner.
However, you should nonetheless try to remember the major
details of your story and not expect to be able to read from a
diary or script when telling your story.

No Hearsay

**Secondly, if you did not witness something directly or only
know about something from a second hand source, then**

you must have the person who has direct knowledge of the event or fact in the hearing room to tell the EAT/Rights Commissioner themselves directly.

Hearsay evidence is not allowed. This means that you are saying in court what you heard from someone else who is not in court. This is very unfair to an employer as he or she will not be able to deny the truth of what you say. Similarly, if the employer is doing this to you, you should object to the Rights Commissioner/EAT about this. This is also a good reason why it is important to tell your lawyers about any witnesses you may have and to have your witnesses available and ready for the hearing itself. It is also a good reason to have any documents you are going to rely on ready for the case. If the witness is not willing to attend voluntarily, you or your lawyer can apply to the EAT before the hearing date for a *subpoena*. This is dealt with below.

Questions from the Judges

Once you have overcome the above obstacles and are now telling your story, you must also be prepared to answer questions from the judges as you are telling your story. You must answer them as accurately as possible. You must also remember that these judges are deciding your case so, even though their questions might seem "off the point" or unrelated to what you are saying, you must still answer them courteously as they are clearly relevant to the judges asking them.

Your Demeanour

Remember also that your demeanour may be watched by the judges.

For example, if the employer claims that you were dismissed for gross misconduct for bullying or aggression and you appear aggressive or hostile when you speak in front of the judges, you will be helping the employer even if what he or she is saying about you is untrue.

For this reason, also, you must remain formal and courteous at all times.

Cross-Examination

After you have told your story and have answered any questions from the judges, you will then be asked questions by the employer or his lawyer. This is called "Cross-Examination".

As a result of the hearing before the Rights Commissioner or the T2 document submitted by the employer before the EAT hearing, you will now know generally what the employer is saying and how he or she is defending the case. This will help you prepare your case before the EAT.

Witness Credibility

It is important to remember that if the employer is right about something, you should say so. This is because if you attack or deny the employer on everything and you are found to be wrong, then this will undermine your story in other parts even if you are correct.

This is called "Witness Credibility" and is an important way that the EAT decides who is telling the truth.

If you are found to have been incorrect in your evidence, then the EAT may draw negative conclusions about whether you are telling the truth about other parts of your story. It is often the case that there will be often no documents or written evidence to give to the EAT/Rights Commissioner and the evidence will be "your word against the employer's".

If you are found to lack credibility, you may lose your case even if you are telling the truth. The EAT decides on the "balance of probabilities" who is telling the truth about what happened and whether what happened amounts to an unfair dismissal. The "balance of probabilities" means who is more likely to be telling the truth. Even if there are doubts about some of the evidence, the EAT will decide what is more likely to have happened even if they never fully establish all the facts with certainty.

Therefore, you must remember that how you present yourself and the evidence is very important indeed.

You must remember that it is also open to the employer to appeal the determination of the Rights Commissioner/EAT. If the employer does appeal, you must be careful to comply with all the documentation you receive from the courts about your case. You cannot take the attitude that you have won your case and now you can do nothing. You must also ensure you attend at all the hearings.

Dates and Adjournments Before the EAT

This issue is far more likely to affect the EAT than the Rights Commissioner. If you are representing yourself, you must be very careful to inform the EAT when you are sending in the T1-A form at first instance or replying to the employer appeal of any dates that are not convenient for you to attend.

Warning!
This is because the EAT does not grant adjournments except in the most limited circumstances and for good reason. An adjournment means postponing the hearing of your case to a different, later date than the one you have been given.

Obviously, situations can arise that were unforeseen at the time you sent in the T1-A form or the appeal form. However, if you are not able to attend the hearing on the date allocated to you, you must immediately inform the Secretariat and will probably have to attend at the EAT yourself to make an application before an actual Tribunal hearing to tell them why you cannot attend.

You must remember that the employer also has rights in the course of the hearing and the Tribunal will be mindful to be fair to him or her.

If you are seeking an adjournment of the hearing, it is strongly advisable that you inform the employer in writing that you are doing so and seek their consent for any new dates you are suggesting.

If the employer consents in writing to a new date, then the EAT may be more willing to give an adjournment. However, it is entirely at the discretion of the Tribunal and they may refuse if they feel that the reason you are giving them for the adjournment is not acceptable.

As such, it is vital that you inform the EAT at the start of the whole process of any dates that are not convenient.

If you have engaged a solicitor, the solicitor or someone from his or her office may go into the EAT and make this application for you. However, this also does not, by any means, guarantee that the adjournment will be granted. You should inform your solicitor as early as you can of any dates you know that are inconvenient for you.

What Happens Prior to the EAT Hearing

It is important to remember that a hearing does not "just happen". As soon as you send in your T1-A document to the EAT secretariat, you set in motion a very important procedure. This procedure exists in order to ensure that both sides to the dispute are ready and know generally what to expect for the hearing date.

When the EAT Secretariat receives your T1-A document, they will send it to the employer at the address you have given in that document. The employer then replies to your claim in his or her own document called a T2 document.

Normally, the employer will deny your version of events and provide his version of events. Many employers will take legal advice before sending this document to the EAT, as they must be very careful not to compromise their defence by any mistakes or concessions they make in filling out the T2. The employer will send this document to the EAT Secretariat directly and the EAT will then forward this document to you.

If the employer does not reply, then technically he or she is not entitled to be heard at the hearing of the claim except with the discretion of the EAT. However, in practice, in the interests of fairness, unless there is some fundamental prejudice to you, the employee, if the employer turns up at the hearing of the claim on the allotted date, without having submitted a T2, the EAT will allow him or her to participate in the hearing.

However, if they do not have a good excuse for not sending in a T2, it creates an early bad impression of the employer for the EAT judges.

Do I Need Lawyers?

No, you do not need to engage lawyers in order to bring an unfair dismissal claim. Indeed, anyone can represent you or assist you at the hearing. However, you should make sure that they are capable of doing a good job for you.

If you have engaged a solicitor, then the solicitor himself or herself will represent you or they, on your instructions, can, in turn, engage a barrister to present the case for you and your solicitor. You can see from what you read above in this Chapter that presenting the case before the EAT is not as simple as you maybe thought and sometimes employees like to engage a barrister who has skills in presenting court cases. Your solicitor might suggest someone to you or you may have your own idea as to who you want.

Alternatively, there are now many solicitors who are skilled in presenting these cases themselves.

No Legal Costs Awarded

When engaging a legal team, employees must be aware that

they are not awarded their legal costs in the event that they succeed or settle their case. This means that the costs of your legal team will be deducted from the award of money you receive from your case.

This makes the decision to take a case at all or to hire lawyers an economic decision based on the return you hope potentially to make from the case. This will be dealt with later.

The great advantage of lawyers is that they can help advise you how to prepare your case and will present your case. If you hire lawyers with experience of employment law matters, they will also know the strengths and weaknesses of your case and will be able to present your case in a way that helps the EAT understand the unlawful nature of your treatment by your employer.

You are now aware that there is a certain skill and discretion involved in presenting a case. The employee may feel that certain events that happened are important but the EAT may disagree. The employee may feel that it is necessary to go through every single incident or evidence. The EAT may disagree. Moreover, the Tribunal members may be constantly assessing their view of the evidence and of the credibility of the parties depending on what they hear in the course of the hearing. Good lawyers are experienced at reading the adjudicators to see what evidence they should prioritise or what arguments to make. This is an important point to remember whether you hire a lawyer or not. Moreover, good employment lawyers will be before the EAT quite regularly and may know the "form" of the individual panel judges.

Consultations

If you hire a solicitor or solicitor and barrister ("the lawyers"), there will normally be at least two consultations.

The **first consultation** will normally be at the initial stage of the case. At this consultation, the lawyers will need to know the details of the case. This will normally be a precise consultation and all relevant information must be disclosed to the lawyers. This is vital as otherwise they will not be prepared for any weakness in your case that the employer may use against you. Also, it will allow the lawyers to prepare the case and decide how to present it.

What Will Happen At My Consultation?

The lawyers will take detailed notes of your claim.

Before this consultation, you should check all your dates and have all relevant documents and information available.

Also, you should be able to tell the lawyers of any available witnesses. This is the case even if you think that the witnesses would not agree to attend on your behalf.

Also, you should be able to tell your lawyers if there is any relevant information that you do not have that you believe that the employer has in his or her possession.

After this consultation, the lawyers will be in a better position to prepare an **Advice on Proofs**. This is a document, normally prepared by a barrister, that sets out the strengths and weaknesses of the case and how much the lawyers believe the case is worth in terms of compensation. However, even if there is a solicitor representing you, he or she will then similarly prepare your case based on this consultation.

Subpoenas

In particular, there is a procedure before the EAT that allows parties to *subpoena* either witnesses or documents from the other side. This application must be made prior to the hearing, and within a reasonable time to allow an employer comply with any order you wish the EAT to make.

This application, if successful, will compel the employer to attend at the hearing with the documents and/or witnesses sought to be examined. It is important to remember that if you *subpoena* a witness, then they are your witness. This means that you cannot cross-examine or treat them in a hostile way. You must accept their evidence and cannot suggest that they are dishonest. This is a technical rule. Similarly, if an order is made against you by the employer, you must comply with this.

As well as any witnesses that you need to *subpoena* ("compel") to attend, you may have your own witnesses who want to give evidence for you.

After the first consultation, these must be contacted to request them to attend on your behalf.

Data Protection and Freedom of Information Acts

You should also seek any relevant information for your case from the Data Protection Commissioner and the Freedom of Information Commissioner. Data Protection covers all workplaces but Freedom of Information only covers public/ semi-state sector employers.

Settlements

At some stage in the course of your unfair dismissal claim, you or your lawyers will consider whether to settle your claim before the hearing.

A settlement means that you enter into agreement with the employer that you will withdraw and end your claim in return for some offer from the employer that you are happy to accept.

Normally, employees are concerned with a financial settlement in order to agree to do this. However, as well as money, other conditions often agreed are that the employer will furnish a basic reference to the employee or that disputed property may be exchanged between the parties.

Also, you may wish to return to the workplace and be reinstated in your job. A settlement can happen at two stages.

Firstly, it can happen before the hearing date and before any of the parties attend at the Tribunal to give evidence.

Secondly, it can happen on the date of the hearing itself prior to the parties going into the Tribunal room to give evidence. This type of settlement is often referred to as happening "on the steps of the court" or as "an out of court settlement". You must give very careful consideration to whether you wish to settle and, if so, at what price.

If the settlement occurs before the hearing date, the employer may communicate with you or your lawyer by correspondence or by telephone. It is often the case in Ireland, that one solicitor will pick up the phone to another solicitor to discuss the case and, if instructed by his client, to offer a settlement figure. If you have engaged a solicitor, he will not commit you to anything during any such discussions with the employer. He will inform you fully of what was said to him, what the figure is that has been offered and if, in his view, this is a reasonable amount.

If you have not engaged a solicitor, it makes it harder for this type of pre-hearing settlement to be entered into as an employer or his lawyers may be more reluctant to approach you directly.

Independent Legal Advice

If you do not have a solicitor for your case and you are offered a settlement figure, you will normally be well advised to obtain **independent legal advice** from a solicitor of your choosing before accepting the settlement.

There are various Free Legal Advice Centres (FLACs) around the country as well as Community and Citizens Advice Bureaux in many cities and towns in Ireland. These offer information and advice in employment law matters, and the FLAC may even arrange for a solicitor and barrister to represent you free of charge. They are under the remit of the State run Legal Aid Board.

You should be most cautious about accepting a settlement on foot of a recommendation from the legal adviser of the employer. This is not to suggest that the employer or the legal team of the employer will act inappropriately, but just to ensure that you are aware of the entirety of your claim and that it is being reflected in the amount being offered.

When Will A Settlement Happen?

On the hearing day, a settlement of the case is also very possible. On many occasions, this type of settlement before the day of the hearing does not arise. Instead, you will be asked by your lawyers or you may decide yourself (if not represented) to attend at the EAT or the Rights Commissioner earlier than the scheduled start time of the hearing. This early arrival allows both sides a little extra time to talk to each other and possibly reach a settlement prior to the start of the hearing itself.

The hearing day will start either in the morning at 10.30am or in the afternoon at 2pm or 2.30pm. All cases are normally listed for half a day. In other words, on the first day of the case, the hearing will run for about two hours only. This means that if the case is a longer one it will not finish on the first day and everyone will have to return for another day on another date to be allocated by the Rights Commissioner or Tribunal. This second date is normally allocated by the Rights Commissioner or the Tribunal at the end of the hearing on the first day.

Also, the Rights Commissioner or Tribunal will try to facilitate both sides of the case. This means that there may be dates that suit you that do not suit the employer or his lawyers and will result in delays to the hearing of the case. Therefore, when you turn up on the first hearing date, you must be aware that this will quite likely not finish on this day.

If you are representing yourself, this may not be a problem. However, when you remember, if you have engaged lawyers, that you will be paying their legal fees for your legal representation on the first hearing day and on subsequent days, it may make the idea of settling the case on the first hearing date more attractive. For example, if you calculate your loss at €10,000 if you win the case, you could lose a lot of that award if the length of time to fight the case increases legal costs greatly. Therefore, the quicker the case ends or the quicker the settlement, the more money you are likely to receive into your hand at the end of the legal case.

Calculating Legal Costs

Given that legal costs are not awarded to you if you win your claim, legal costs are quite expensive for employment cases and should always be discussed with your solicitor in advance of the case. There is no set scale of fees and depends on the nature of the case and the amount of work involved. A barrister will also charge legal costs and this will include the costs of all work done at consultations, all paperwork, all correspondence, attendance at the first hearing and a refresher fee for all attendances at subsequent hearing if the case does not finish on the first day.

Since you will not be awarded your legal costs by the Rights Commissioner or EAT in the event that you are successful, a settlement is a very wise move to consider at the initial stage of the case even if the money you are offered before the hearing is not fully what you hope to obtain if you win the case as the legal costs in winning the case outright after a full hearing may take a huge chunk out of that award anyway.

If you are found to have brought the unfair dismissal claim in a frivolous or vexatious way, it is open to the employer to penalise you by seeking an order that you pay the expenses of his witnesses for attendance at the hearing. However, this is very rarely ordered by the Rights Commissioner of EAT.

PART C: HOW THE DAY MAY UNFOLD

Starting The Day

Meeting Everyone

As such, if you take a typical start time of 10.30am, your solicitor may normally arrange to meet you and your witnesses at 9am or 9.30am. If there are rooms in the Tribunal building, you can meet there. Often you may arrange to meet your solicitors at a coffee shop or hotel in the vicinity of the Rights Commissioner or Employment Appeals Tribunal hearing. This can happen because, if you are outside of Dublin, the Rights Commissioner or EAT hearing may be held in a local hotel. However, the EAT, in particular, has hearings increasingly in local court houses. You may rightly find this intimidating given that the EAT is supposed to be more informal and not a formal type of court case but this can happen unfortunately.

Your Consultation

As you meet your solicitor and possibly barrister, you may notice your former employer and his legal team nearby. This is not something to feel worried by. It simply means that they are also talking about how to handle the case and possibly even settling it. Normally, at this **pre-hearing consultation** (normally your second consultation with the lawyers following on from the first consultation when you gave them all the details to prepare the case), you will update your lawyers on any information that you were not sure of before at the first consultation.

Your Witnesses

You may also introduce to them some or all of **your witnesses**. If you have any new documents or correspondence, this is the time to give them to the legal team as otherwise it may be too late.

Your Booklet of Pleadings

Ideally, all documents, records and correspondence should already be furnished to your lawyers. This is because they have to prepare a "Booklet of Pleadings" for you. If you are representing yourself, you should also prepare one. This is simply a booklet bound and containing with page numbers all the documents you wish to show the Rights Commissioner or EAT judges during the hearing. "Pleadings" simply means arguments that you are going to make.

If you are before the EAT, five copies of this Booklet should be prepared: one for yourself, one for each of the three Tribunal panel members and one for the employer.

If you are before the Rights Commissioner, then 3 copies will suffice: 1 for yourself, 1 for the employer and 1 for the Rights Commissioner.

Considering the Settlement Offer

In the course of the talking with your lawyer before the hearing, you may decide to approach the other side to see if they are interested in settling the claim. Alternatively, the other side may approach you for this purpose. At this point, you should take all personal animosity out of the affair and look on the business aspects of the decision to settle.

In particular, you must listen to any advice you are getting from your lawyers about what is reasonable to expect if you succeed. Sometimes, you may not agree with your legal team but remember that even if you fight the case and come out with a bit more money, the legal costs of fighting the case for a longer time will have to come out of that amount and you may come out with less overall. As such, you must seek to maximise your return.

Normally, a settlement works by the two set of lawyers going off to talk separately to each other away from their clients and then returning to their clients with the result of their discussions.

There will be **an initial offer** of compensation. If you reject this initial offer, you must be able to identify the amount you are looking for. Normally, you will pitch your case in a settlement at it highest point. This means that, if everything went perfectly for you at the hearing, you put the largest amount you hope to get from the case in this situation to the employer. In reality, unfortunately, nothing works perfectly. As such, you must be aware that once you are in the hearing room before the judges, if you do not settle, what you thought they would support or believe about your case, they may reject or ignore and the value of the case goes down drastically. All court cases are high risk. As such, you may be willing to come down from your highest pitch depending on what the particular risks of your case might be and also to reduce legal costs.

Once you instruct your lawyer to make **a replying offer** ("counter-offer") to the employer, the employer will need time to think about it. He may then send his legal team back to your lawyer and they will again go away to talk to each other. The employer lawyer will normally make another offer in response to your offer that is lower that what you requested and the whole process of offer and counter-offer may start again.

This "toing and froing" will continue until either there is no hope of a common figure, acceptable to both sides being agreed, or until a figure is indeed agreed. The figure acceptable to you is unique to your case and based on recommendations from your lawyers.

If they feel that time may facilitate a successful settlement, the EAT or Rights Commissioner will normally put back the start of the hearing for a reasonable period of time.

However, after about 30 minutes from the scheduled start of the hearing, they will normally insist on commencing the hearing. All settlement discussions are confidential and what is said by the lawyers outside of court cannot be used against each other in the hearing itself. As such, the Tribunal judges will not know the extent to which either side was willing to settle the case or the reasons why. Of course, in the course of the hearing, they will discover these things for themselves.

Indeed, it is quite common for a Rights Commissioner or an EAT, after hearing some evidence, to stop the hearing for a period of time, to request the parties again try to settle the case. This sometimes is a strong hint to an employee that he may not win his case if it proceeds and that he should try and give another chance at a settlement.

Putting the Settlement Terms into Writing

If a settlement is reached, it must be put down in writing precisely on paper. It is normally handwritten outside the door of the court and typed up later when everyone is back in the office.

- It must be dated and the full title of the case with its reference number must be put on to the document containing the terms of the settlement.
- Most importantly, a settlement of an unfair dismissal case is normally a full and final settlement of all claims that may arise out of the employment relationship with the employer. Therefore, the money you accept should reflect the fact that you may have other claims outstanding such as a personal injury claim, a health and safety claim or an equality claim.
- The settlement document is then signed by you and witnessed by your solicitor or some other witness.

- You must read this document carefully before signing and, if you have lawyers, listen carefully to their advice. After you sign the document, the case is settled.

The lawyers will go into the Rights Commissioner or Tribunal room and inform the Commissioner or Tribunal that the case is settled. At this stage, you may decide not to go in with them to the hearing room. The Commissioner or EAT will then adjourn the matter for approximately one month to allow the settlement to be carried out, namely, the paying over of the money by the employer or the carrying out of any other terms like reinstatement or the supplying of a reference. Once the settlement is carried out, on the expiry of the adjournment date, your case will be struck out by the EAT/Rights Commissioner and comes to an end.

Warning!
If the settlement has not been carried out by the adjournment date, you should ensure to be in attendance at the EAT/Rights Commissioner to apply that your case be re-listed for a new hearing date.

The Hearing Room

If a settlement is not reached, then you must now prepare yourself for the hearing and entering the hearing room. When you walk into the hearing room, you will notice that there are tables and chairs set out in a business like manner usually with a top table and two other tables facing each other across the room.

For the tables facing each other, one table is for you and your legal team (if you have engaged one) and the other table opposite you is for the employer and his legal team (if he or she has engaged one). Depending on where you have opted to go, the top table is either for the Rights Commissioner or the

Employment Appeals Tribunal judges. The difference between the two is that if you are before a Right Commissioner only one person will sit at the top table. If you are before the EAT, there will be four people at the top table. This is explained in more detail below.

Normally, there will also be a fourth table in the room. This is a table right in front of the top table where you will sit when you give evidence about your case. In other words, you will have to sit in the centre of the room in front of the judges.

Also, if you are living outside of Dublin, most EAT hearings are held in hotels in accordance with the above layout, although sometimes the EAT hearing is held in a court room and you will find yourself in a court setting including a witness box.

If you are in Dublin, there are designated offices and hearing rooms from which the Rights Commissioner Service and the Employment Appeals Tribunal operate. If you are going to the Rights Commissioner in the Dublin area, you will normally be attending a hearing at the offices of the Labour Relations Commissioner, Haddington Road, Dublin 4. If you are attending a hearing at the Employment Appeals Tribunal in the Dublin area, you will normally be travelling to Davitt House, Adelaide Road, Dublin 2. If you are outside the Dublin area, the Rights Commissioner and the Employment Appeals Tribunal will be travelling to your area and will normally take up their work in a local hotel laid out for the event or even in a local court house.

You should always make sure you know where your case is going to be held before the hearing date. All these details will be provided to you in correspondence in the lead up to the hearing confirming the date and the location of the hearing. This correspondence will come either from the Rights Commissioner Service of the Labour Relations Commission or the Employment Appeals Tribunal Secretariat. You must also start a file for your case and ensure to keep and store all correspondence received in this file.

Once you have arrived:

    (a) At the correct location;
    (b) on the correct date;
    (c) at the time you were advised by your lawyers or an hour before the hearing in the event that you might consider a settlement; and
    (d) no settlement has been reached,

you will now find yourself in the hearing room.

As set out above, there will only be one person at the top table if you are before a Rights Commissioner. If you sit in front of the EAT, there will be four people at the top table. When you walk into the room, the top table will be empty. The employer side will normally be already sitting down or enter the room after you. The Rights Commissioner or the EAT "Panel" will normally wait for every body to be seated in the room before entering themselves.

As a traditional mark of respect for the position of these adjudicators, when the Rights Commissioner or the EAT Panel enter the room you stand up. As they leave the room, you do the same. The roots of the Irish legal system are ancient and based on respect for the authority of the judge. This may seem very deferential in modern times but you must remember that these judges whether the Rights Commissioner or the EAT are not just individuals. They are representing the Irish legal system itself. For this reason, you will understand that this respect for the judges is really respect for the legal system itself and values it embodies. For this reason also, when speaking to the Rights Commissioner and the EAT you should always be very respectful.

If you are in front of the Right Commissioner, unless told otherwise, you should address him or her formally by their surname using "Mr" or "Ms". If you are before the EAT, if you are speaking to the Chairperson of the panel, you should refer to him or her as Mr Chairman or Madam Chairperson. If you are speaking to the other two members of the panel, you should refer to them in the same way as a Rights Commissioner above. You may hear some lawyers, usually barristers, refer to the panel as "Sir" or "Madam". This is perhaps a little too formal and not required.

We already set out above the rest of the nature of the Rights Commissioner hearing. This can be very informal and less complicated than the EAT. As such, we will now look at the running of the EAT hearing in particular.

The Adjudicators

There will be 3 EAT Judges. These are not technically judges in the traditional sense. They are known as the EAT "Panel" hearing your case.

- The Chairperson of this Panel will be a practising barrister or solicitor.
- Another person on the panel will be drawn from a trade union background.
- The third person on the Panel will be drawn from an Employer background.

There will be 4 persons on the Panel. This is the Registrar. They are responsible for the organisation of the hearing itself. The person who is Registrar for your hearing will normally meet you before the meeting and take the details of your name and the names of your legal team. He or she will also inform you who is the Chairperson allocated to hear your case and at what time they propose to start. It is at this point that the Registrar may enquire whether you are seeking some time "to talk" to the other side. This means that the EAT Registrar is enquiring whether you might be in a position to settle your case and avoid a hearing. As set out above, this is a normal part of the litigation process and can be very beneficial to claimants.

Opening the Case

If you do not settle the claim and are now sitting in the EAT, the next step is that the EAT panel will enter the room and take their seats along with the Registrar at the top table. Once they are seated, they will introduce themselves individually. If you have lawyers, you may now notice that they commence to take notes of what is being said. If you do not have a legal team, you should have a notepad and pen in front of you along with your Booklet of Pleadings (see above) and start to take a careful note of what is said.

You should take a note of the names of the Adjudicators so that you know what to call them in reply to any of their questions. The adjudicators are aware that this is a stressful situation for you so if you forget things like their names, of course, they do not mind.

What the Adjudicators on the Panel do next is important. They start the hearing by going down through the T1-A document you have submitted and the T2 document submitted by the employer.

In short, the EAT Panel want to make sure that they have the power to hear the claim and that the basic details of the employment relationship are correct and *agreed by both sides*.

This is done by the Rights Commissioner at the start of his hearing also. If you can agree the basic details of the employment relationship with the other side before the start of the hearing, this will greatly speed up matters and facilitate the adjudicators. Details that must be as correct as possible and preferably agreed are:

(a) The start of the employment contract;
(b) the date of termination of the employment contract;
(c) gross remuneration (wages) per week (if variable, an average to include basic salary and other work related benefits); and

(d) nett remuneration per week (if variable, an average to include basic salary and other work related benefits);

The Rights Commissioner/EAT will also inquire whether the dismissal is in dispute.

What this means is whether the employer accepts that he or she dismissed you or whether the employer is stating that you resigned from your work of your own choice. This will normally be stated by the employer in his defence T2 Form, so you should know in advance if this issue is going to be raised by your employer. This issue is very important as to how the case will be conducted by the Tribunal or Rights Commissioner.

The details about the start and commencement dates are relevant to whether you have the necessary 52 weeks' continuous service in order to bring a claim. The details about your salary are relevant to the possible financial compensation you may receive if you are successful.

Finally, the EAT/Rights Commissioner will inquire about other claims you might be asking them to make a decision on along with the unfair dismissal claim. For example, as well as compensation for the dismissal, the Rights Commissioner or the EAT can also award you any unpaid or untaken holiday leave entitlements prior to the dismissal and any pay for your notice period that you were not given. The Claim Form (T1-A Form) for your unfair dismissal claim will allow you seek compensation for these issues also and you must make sure that these claims are marked on your unfair dismissal claim form. If not, you may not be allowed to seek this additional compensation during your unfair dismissal claim.

Preliminary Points

Sometimes, it is genuinely not possible to agree these details with the employer before the hearing as this may be part of the dispute between the parties that the EAT/Rights Commissioner must decide.

As such, if the details are very relevant to the claim, the EAT/Rights Commissioner might treat them as "a preliminary point". This means that this point or issue is so important to the outcome of the case that the EAT/Rights Commissioner decides to hear arguments from both sides about this issue first.

For example, if there is a dispute about when you started employment with your employer, this may seem a small detail to you but it may affect whether you have 52 weeks' continuous service with your employer in order to allow you to bring a claim in the first place.

As such, the EAT/Rights Commissioner must hear arguments about this issue first as otherwise they will not have authority (referred to as "jurisdiction") to hear the rest of your case at all. You will also be called to give your version of events in the witness box or at the "witness table", as will the employer. You or your lawyers will be able to challenge the employer's version of events and the employer or his lawyers will be able to challenge your version. The issue of presenting your case and challenging the employer's case is dealt with above.

This means you and your lawyers must be ready to deal with this "preliminary point" from the start of the hearing rather than expect to be able to deal with it later in the hearing or deal with the main part of your case immediately. This is another factor that may delay the length of time it will take to hear your case and may make legal costs higher.

As such, if there is a dispute of this nature affecting your case, it is another factor that you should consider if you are thinking about a settlement of your case.

Sometimes, also the Rights Commissioner/EAT may give the parties another opportunity to settle after the hearing of the case has begun. This can happen, in particular, when there is a preliminary point in the case. This is because the employer and the employee are now aware that the case may drag on for much longer than expected or, depending on the decision of the Rights Commissioner/EAT on the preliminary point, that they may actually lose the case.

Sometimes, the Rights Commissioner/EAT will leave the room for a period of time to discuss and decide on the preliminary point. During this time, the EAT/Rights Commissioner is said to have "risen". This time allows any further confidential discussions to occur between the parties to the dispute. Before rising, the EAT/Rights Commissioner may remind the parties of how important the preliminary point is to the outcome of their case and the consequences of a negative finding for them. This may cause you and the employer to consider the possibility of settling your case while the EAT/Rights Commissioner has risen to make a decision.

Who Goes First?

If you have gotten over all of these obstacles and there are no further difficulties, the EAT/Rights Commissioner will normally want to go immediately into evidence. This means that they want to hear both sides' version of events.

There are now two possible scenarios.

> *Firstly, if the employer does not deny that he dismissed you but is arguing that the dismissal is fair, he or she will go through and present his or her evidence first.*

This means that the employer and his or her witnesses will be called one after another into "the witness box" to go through their evidence. If they have a lawyer, they will first be answering questions given to them by their own lawyer. This is called "examination". After each of these witnesses has finished, you or your lawyer may then question them. You must put your version of events to each of them in turn and ask questions of them that undermine their story or support your version of events. This is called "cross-examination".

If you do not put your version of events to the employer's witnesses and allow them to respond to it, you may be stopped from making those arguments later in the hearing during your evidence. This is because the EAT seeks to be fair to both sides.

You put your version of events to the employer in the following way:

Suppose there is a dispute about whether or not a meeting was held on a particular date and the employer is now being cross examined by the employee or his lawyer before the EAT, the following questions might unfold:

> **Employee:** "*It will be my evidence that this meeting took place on December 5. If it is the case that you now say this meeting happened on December 10, how can you explain this email I received from you on December 8, referring to "our recent meeting?"*"

> **Employer**: "*Yes. I can see where the confusion arises. But, I am positive that this meeting happened on December 10 and the reference in my email to our "recent meeting" is actually referring to that meeting coming up on the 10th. Maybe I used the wrong word in my email and should have been more precise and said 'our upcoming meeting' but I did not realise that my emails would end up in court.*"

> **Employee**: "*So you are saying that you made a mistake in your email. However, it is my claim that this meeting did happen on the 5th, that there is no mistake in your email and I will be calling my witnesses later in the hearing to prove it.*"

You will notice that the first sentence of the first question of the employee is where the employee *puts his version of the events* to the employer before he asks his own question. By doing this, he is being fair to the employer and will be able to now present evidence that the meeting happened on December 5 later in the hearing by calling witnesses. If the employee or his lawyer does not do this, there may be a risk that the employer will object to your evidence on the basis that he was not told about it and was not given a opportunity to deny it during his own questioning.

A process like this continues in this way until the employer and all the witnesses for the employer have been dealt with. It is only at this point that you and your witnesses will be called to give your evidence.

Depending on the number of witnesses and the complexity of the case, this process can take some time. Most EAT cases are listed for "half a day". This is approximately 2 hours. Therefore, it is often the case that an employee leaves an EAT hearing on the first day without even starting their own case.

> *Secondly, if the employer denies that he dismissed you and is claiming that you resigned of your own choice, then the dismissal is contested and you, as the employee, must go first.*

If you claim you were forced out of your employment by intolerable working conditions or unreasonable treatment at the hands of your employer, this is called a "constructive dismissal". If the dismissal is denied, you will give your evidence first and, if you have a lawyer, he or she will ask you questions to take you through your story first.

Warning!
However, your lawyer cannot give factual evidence him or herself directly for you and relies on you to give the story to the EAT. This is your "examination."

You should never ever change your story from the version of events given by you to your lawyer in advance of the hearing. After you have answered the questions of your own lawyer, you will then be "cross-examined" by the employer or his lawyer. This process will continue until both you and all your witnesses have been examined and cross-examined. Then, the process will start again with the employer and his witnesses. Again, this process is likely to take more than "half a day" and is likely to result in you having to return for a second hearing date.

Second Hearing Dates

If your case goes into a second hearing day, this means that you have to return to the EAT (normally Rights Commissioners finish in one day) on a further second occasion. Indeed, if it is a very complex case, you may have to return on more than one occasion.

However, the EAT will only allow this where the case warrants such a lengthy hearing. Unnecessarily complicated evidence or irrelevant details will not normally cause the EAT to extend the hearing into a longer type of hearing.

However, it is quite common for an average unfair dismissal claim that does not settle to now go into a second day. As you approach the end of the first hearing date (approximately 1pm if you had a 10.30am start and 5pm for a 2.30pm start), the EAT will break at a convenient time in the evidence such as the end of the examination and cross-examination of one particular witness.

The Registrar who is also sitting at the top table then

becomes the important person in the room. He will have a diary of available EAT dates. The EAT Panel Chairperson will enquire from both sides of their availability for a further hearing date. When a date suitable to both sides and the EAT panel itself is agreed, the case will stand adjourned until the next hearing date.

Normally, there is a break of about two months between the first hearing date and the second available hearing date. Also, it will be the same EAT Panel that will be present for the second hearing date. The period of time between the hearing dates may again be used to explore the possibility of a settlement of the case.

Calculation and Mitigation of Loss

Having gone through the evidence of what happened to you and your employer's defence as to what happened, the EAT and the Rights Commissioner will then hear evidence as to what you say you have suffered financially as a result of the dismissal. This is normally done near the end of the hearing.

It is important to have a Schedule of Loss in your Booklet of Pleadings of your *actual loss* to date and any *ongoing (future) losses*.

Your actual loss would be the amount of weeks you were out of work without a salary. This was dealt with above earlier.

An *ongoing (future) loss* would be where you have secured a new job but at a lesser rate of remuneration than the old job from which you were dismissed.

Again, included in the concept of remuneration is not only basic salary but also other work-related benefits that you have now lost such as pension contributions or bonuses.

If there is any variation in aspects of salary such as performance related bonuses, then you should be able to provide an average figure based on past amounts for the purpose of calculating your loss of salary. Issues such as inconvenience, embarrassment, defamation or distress are not subject to compensation before the Rights Commissioner or the EAT.

However, in order to recover the full amount of compensation you seek, you must also show the Rights Commissioner/EAT that you sought *to mitigate your loss*.

This means that you sought to find alternative employment during your period of unemployment in order to reduce the loss you have suffered. If you are still unemployed at the time of the EAT/Rights Commissioner hearing, then you must be particularly careful to be able to show that you tried to find alternative employment prior to the hearing.

In particular, you must have documents to hand into the EAT/Rights Commissioner in your Booklet of Pleadings showing all the job applications you have made and any responses or results to those job applications. If you are still unemployed at the time of the hearing and you cannot show the EAT/Rights Commissioner what you have done to find a new job, then you may suffer a loss in the amount of compensation you might otherwise have received for your financial loss.

Determinations

After your case is heard, the EAT/Rights Commissioner will end the hearing and leave the hearing room. They will then take a number of weeks to discuss the case and draw up a decision called a "*determination*". This normally takes 8 to 10 weeks to receive this decision and will be sent to you or, if you have engaged one, a solicitor. This will state whether you have been successful, the reasoning for the determination and, if successful, the financial compensation or other redress (re-instatement or re-engagement) that is ordered.

Appeal from the EAT and Enforcement of Awards

You will have six weeks from the date that the determination was communicated to you to bring an appeal to the Circuit Court (see Chapter 3 of this Book).

At this point, if you decide to appeal, you enter the formal court process of the Circuit Court for the area you are in. The Circuit, High and Supreme Court are referred to as the Civil Courts. For example, if your employer lives or is based in Dublin, your appeal will be to the Dublin Circuit Court. Your employer can also appeal. In the event that your employer does not appeal but has not complied with the EAT determination, you or your lawyers can bring enforcement proceedings against him or her in Circuit Court. The area of bringing your claim to the Civil Courts is dealt with later in this book.

Equality

PART A: ARE YOU PROTECTED?

What Are The Grounds of Your Claim?

The relevant law in this area is called the Employment Equality Act 1998-2004. Every claim is different and will have different facts. For this reason, many people will engage a solicitor in order to pursue their case. However, most workplace discrimination cases fall within the general headings set out now in the following:

"Discrimination"

There are 9 characteristics of every person which are protected against Discrimination under Irish law. These are:

- Marital Status.
- Age.
- Sexual Orientation.
- Family Status.
- Race.
- Gender.
- Religious belief.
- Disability.
- Membership of the Travelling Community.

If you fall within 1 or more of these 9 characteristics, discrimination at work occurs where:

(a) A person is treated less favourably than

another person is, has been or would be treated in a comparable situation on the basis of one of the above grounds. This means that you must compare yourself to someone else in the workplace who does not fall within 1 of the above 9 grounds. However, you do not have to actually show that someone in a comparable situation to you is currently working in the workplace and is being treated differently. The Labour Court, Equality Tribunal and Circuit Court can compare you to people who worked for the same employer in the past and who were treated differently to you. They can even create their own an employee who does not exist in reality and compare you to that employee. This is referred to as the "hypothetical employee".

(b) Also, a person can bring a claim of discrimination where they do not actually have one of the relevant 9 characteristics if the person discriminating against them *wrongly believes* that they have it.

(c) A person can bring a discrimination claim not because they fall within 1 of the 9 above grounds or that the discriminator thinks they do but because they are *associated or have become friends* with someone in the workplace who does have one of the above nine characteristics and they are treated less favourably as a result of this association or friendship.

Who Is Protected?

The protection against discrimination is very wide-ranging. The following categories of person are protected:

(a) Agency workers;
(b) Employees;
(c) Self-Employed persons and Independent Contractors;
(d) Partners in a partnership;
(e) People on vocational type training in a workplace.

In order to show that you are being less favourably treated, you have to compare yourself to someone within your *specific type of employment*.

This means that if you are a worker allocated to a workplace by a recruitment agency, you are supposed to compare yourself only to other agency workers in the same workplace.

Similarly, if you are an independent contractor or self-employed person in the workplace, you are only supposed to compare yourself to other independent contractors there and to the actual employees of that business. In other words, you are not supposed to compare yourself to full employees of the employer if you are not an employee of that employer yourself.

However, you can avoid this restriction through the use of the "**hypothetical comparator**" mentioned above. This means that, even if you are the only agency worker in the workplace, although you technically have no other agency worker to compare yourself to, the courts can make up a hypothetical agency worker and base the characteristic of this hypothetical worker on the way full employees of the employer are treated.

For example, suppose you are the only female agency worker in an all male workplace and there are no actual male agency workers there, the courts can nonetheless create a hypothetical male agency worker to which to compare you based on the way the other men in the workplace are being treated even though those other men are full employees of the business and not agency workers themselves.

What Is Protected?

The situations covered are very wide ranging. All less favourable treatment on 1 of the above 9 grounds in relation to:

> (a) **Access** to Employment and Job Interviews.
> (b) Terms and conditions of your contract of employment including pay.
> (c) Promotion, training, allocation of responsibilities.
> (d) The application of the Disciplinary and Grievance policy and procedure.
> (e) **Dismissal** and termination of employment.

It is very important to remember that there is one big difference between the equality rights in this Chapter and the unfair dismissal claims in Chapter 1.

You can bring an equality claim at any time in your employment, and you do not have to wait until you have 52 weeks' continuous service with your employer.

In other words, if you have only worked for an employer for one month and you are dismissed, you can bring a dismissal claim under the equality legislation in this Chapter, but you would not be able to bring an unfair dismissal claim set out in Chapter 1.

Sexual Harassment

As well as discrimination and dismissal, you are also protected against sexual harassment in the workplace. This is a specific form of protection against discrimination with a sexual motivation. It covers heterosexual and homosexual harassment.

The Location

An employee may be sexually harassed either:

> **In the workplace**; or

> is subjected **outside the workplace** to work-related harassment.

Examples

Physical Conduct of a Sexual Nature

   This conduct may include ***unwanted*** physical contact such as unnecessary:

- Touching.
- Patting.
- Pinching.
- Brushing against another employee's body.
- Assault.
- Coercive sexual intercourse.

It must be remembered that any of these above actions may also amount to a criminal offence against you and you may wish to make a complaint to the police. Your employer must also be informed as soon as possible of any unwanted behaviour of this nature even if outside working hours and how you wish to deal with the matter.

Verbal Conduct of a Sexual Nature

This includes behaviour such as ***unwanted***:

- Sexual advances.
- Propositions.
- Pressure for sexual activity.

- Continued suggestions for social activity outside of the workplace after it has been made clear that such suggestions are unwanted.
- Unwanted or offensive flirtations and suggestive remarks.
- Lewd innuendo and comments.

Non-Verbal Conduct of a Sexual Nature

This may include the display of pornographic or sexually suggestive:

- Pictures.
- Objects.
- Written materials.
- E-mails.
- Faxes
- Mobile telephone text-messages.

Harassment

As well as discrimination, dismissal and sexual harassment, you can also be "harassed" in the workplace. The meaning of "harassment" is the same as that for sexual harassment but without the sexual element. Instead, the harassment has to be based on or motivated by one or more of the nine relevant characteristic of the employee targeted. For example, if you are sexually harassed, it means that you are being offended or pestered sexually. However, if you are harassed, if means that you being bullied because, for example, you are female or disabled even though there is no sexual element to the bullying.

Harassment is any act or conduct including:

- Spoken words,
- gestures, or
- the production, display or circulation of written words, pictures or other material,

if the conduct is unwanted to the employee and has the purpose or effect of violating a person's dignity and creates an intimidatory, hostile, degrading, humiliating or offensive *environment* for the person.

The Location

Again, you may be harassed either:

In the workplace; or

is subjected **outside the workplace** to work-related harassment.

The protection of the Act extends to situations where the employee does not have the relevant characteristic but the **harasser believes** that he or she has that characteristic.

Assumptions

Examples

Where the harasser is a religious bigot who believes that the targeted employee either is of a different faith or denomination or holds *no* religious belief when that is not correct.

When the harasser believes that the employee targeted is gay when he or she is not.

Attributes

Example

An employee is protected when he is harassed not about his

race directly (such as his national or ethnic origin) but about some other physical or social feature referable to belonging to that race such as skin or hair colour, height or accent.

Similarly, a religious belief may not be targeted directly by the harasser, but instead he or she may base the harassment on a dietary regime or dress code associated with and required by it. In this case, an employee is also protected.

Therefore, a wide range of behaviour, when related to 1 or more of the 9 grounds, may constitute harassment. It may include:

- Verbal harassment: Jokes, comments, ridicule or songs.
- Physical harassment: Jostling, shoving or any form of assault.
- Written harassment: Faxes, e-mails, text messages, bulletins or notices.
- Intimidatory harassment: Gestures, posturing or intimidatory poses.
- Isolation or exclusion from social activities.
- Pressure to behave in a manner that the employee thinks is inappropriate. For example, a requirement to dress in a manner acutely unsuited to a person's ethnic or religious background or belief.

Victimisation

You are also protected under the equality legislation against being victimised. You are victimised by your employer when you make a complaint or seek to challenge acts of discrimination or harassment against you in the workplace and, as a result, you are penalised or dismissed from your job. Examples of "penalisation" may be:

(a) Not being promoted as a result of a discrimination claim or complaint;
(b) unreasonable rostering or changes to conditions of employment as a result of a complaint;
(c) being paid differently to workers or not being paid bonuses in circumstances where the way pay or bonuses are calculated is unclear; or
(d) not being made full time or permanent as a result of a previous complaint;

Equal Pay

It is a fundamental principle of Irish law that all workers in comparable employment receive equal pay for equal work or work of equal value.

If not, this is a form of discrimination and may be challenged under the equality legislation by bringing an "equal pay claim." This type of claim started off to protect women but now covers all workers.

For example, if a group of workers are being paid less than Irish workers and it happens that these lesser paid workers are non-Irish, it does not matter what the gender of the workers is as the employer must be able to explain the reasons for this. If there is not lawful or transparent reason, he or she must pay all workers equally and compensate the foreign workers for the time in employment on the lesser rate of pay.

On many occasions, the employer will not discriminate in terms of pay directly. Instead, there may be a criteria or scale of pay affecting workers which, when examined more closely, tends of affect one group of workers more than another and it just happens that the less favourably treated group are, for example, disabled or foreign.

For example, suppose you are a part-time worker and your employer does not offer you a pension package or performance bonus as part of your salary at all even though these are offered to full time workers. If it turns out that most

*of the part-time workers are, for example, disabled or foreign,
then this must also be explained.*

**This is called indirect discrimination and must also be
justified by an employer. If not, again, he or she will be
found in breach of equal pay rules.**

PART B: STARTING THE CASE

Now that you know about when you might have an
employment equality claim, you need to know when and
where to start the claim.

The Equality Tribunal

Since 2004, the Equality Tribunal hears cases of:

(a) Discriminatory or Victimisation Dismissals.
(b) All claims relating to discrimination in regard
     to Occupational Pensions.
(c) Sexual Harassment and Harassment Claims.
(d) Discrimination Claims (not amounting to
     dismissal or harassment).
(e) Equal Pay Claims.

The Circuit Court

Gender Equality

Any of the above claims relating specifically to **gender
equality** can go directly to the Circuit Court.

**Legal costs are awarded under this route to the winning
side.**

Legal Costs

This is a double edged sword as if you win your case you

will be awarded your legal costs on top of the compensation you were awarded. However, if you lose your case and do not receive any compensation, you will be liable to pay the legal costs of your employer as well as those of your own legal team. As such, you must not take the decision to bring your case to the Circuit Court lightly as the financial consequences of failure can be expensive.

No Limit on Compensation Awarded

On the other hand, the Circuit Court, when hearing an equality case, has no limit on the amount of compensation it can award. Awards in the past have been quite high and up to €100,000 and more.

More Formal Procedures

This route, however, is also more formal than the Equality Tribunal route. Your claim must also be set out in a Circuit Court document called a Civil Bill. This is a precise legal document that is normally written up by lawyers. Normally, a solicitor and barrister ("the lawyers") are engaged if you wish to proceed on this route.

Multiple Forms of Protection

What is interesting about this route, however, is the ability to bring different types of claim on the one court document (civil bill). For example, if you being dismissed and you are saying this is related to your gender, you could seek an injunction from the Circuit Court to stop the dismissal until the hearing of the equality claim. An injunction is not available in the Equality Tribunal or Labour Court. Injunctions are discussed later in Chapter 3 of this book.

Appeals

There is a right of appeal from the Equality Tribunal to the Labour Court. This must be brought within 6 weeks of the date of the determination of the Equality Tribunal.

There is a right of appeal from the Circuit Court to the High Court. This also must be brought within 6 weeks of the date of the judgment of the Circuit Court.

Choose the Correct Court

If you have been dismissed, you can only take one dismissal claim. Therefore, you must choose where to take that claim.

A. Unfair Dismissal versus Discriminatory Dismissal

You may take it under the unfair dismissals route as set out in Chapter 1 **or** you may take it under the employment equality route as set out in this Chapter.

However, to bring a dismissal under the Equality legislation, you must show a link to one of the 9 protected grounds.

You cannot take both.

B. Wrongful Dismissal versus Unfair/Discriminatory Dismissal

On the other hand, you may wish to go into the Circuit or High Court and sue your employer for breach of contract for wrongful dismissal (discussed in Chapter 3 of this book). However, again, you **cannot** then take either an unfair or an equality dismissal claim.

C. Equality Law versus Part-Time Worker Law

If you are a part-time worker or a fixed-term worker and have been discriminated against, you also cannot bring two claims for the same events under *both* the employment equality route and either the Protection of Employees (Part-Time Workers) Act 2001. Also, if the discrimination against you also relates to your status as a fixed-term worker, you cannot take two claims for the same acts of discrimination under the equality legislation and the Protection of Employees (Fixed-Term Workers) Act 2003.

You must choose between an equality claim or a claim under these two other statutes.

Reasons For Choosing Different Courts

You must be very careful when choosing where to take your case.

For example, if you decide to go to the Equality Tribunal, you must be able to show that the treatment to which you were subjected was related to one of the nine protected grounds set out above. If you cannot do this, even if you dismissal is found to be unfair (for example, your employer never gave you any warning of your dismissal), you will still lose your case because you cannot show that there was a link to one of the nine discrimination grounds.

There is, however, one entitlement that may help you if you bring a claim under the equality legislation and you find yourself in this situation.

Since 2004, if the Director of the Equality Tribunal considers it appropriate, she may issue a direction permitting the complainant to proceed with their complaint *again* but this time under the Unfair Dismissals Act 1977-2001.

The importance of this is that an employee does not have to show that his dismissal was linked to one of the 9 grounds in the unfair dismissals route and can win his or her case if he can just show that his or her dismissal was unfair.

Nature of Limitation Period

A complaint must be made within 6 months of the date of the last incident of discrimination or dismissal or victimisation.

The date on which a complaint is "made" is the date on which the Tribunal *receives* a completed Complaint Form and not when it sent off by post.

The Tribunal may extend the period for making the complaint from 6 months to a maximum of 12 months from the date of the last incident of discrimination. It can only do so where there is *a reasonable cause* that prevented the making of the complaint within the previous 6 months.

Employer Deceit or Misrepresentations

Where a delay in starting your claim is caused by an employer misrepresenting to you the facts or truth of a case, the date that you lodged your claim with the Equality Tribunal or Circuit Court will be deemed in fact to be date upon which the misrepresentation was made to you. In other words, the employer's lies stop the clock.

The six-month time limit for referring complaints does **not** apply to equal pay cases. These can be brought at any time.

The Claim Form

The employee commences their claim before the Equality Tribunal by filling in a specific document called the **EE1 Form**. This is a pre-printed document available at the Equality Tribunal website: www.equalitytribunal.ie.

It is made up of a number of sections seeking basic information about:

- Your identity,
- your contact address, and
- the name and address of your employer or, if different, the party you are suing.

The latter point is important as you saw earlier in this Chapter that a discrimination claim can be brought against other parties besides an employer.

For example, an independent contractor can sue a business he or she is working for and a partner can sue a partnership even though they are not "employees" of that person.

Therefore, you must make very sure that you are suing the right party as if you make a mistake you may be out of time to begin a claim against the right party.

The Contents of the Form

Part 1 of the EE1 Document seeks your details as the Complainant.

Part Two is a section completed by the Equality Tribunal itself and does not concern you.

Part Three is a section of the Form that requests you to tick the precise ground upon which you are claiming you were discriminated against. There are 9 specific characteristics protected against discrimination and these are set out in this Chapter.

You have to tick the box beside the ground upon which you are relying. You may be claiming that you were discriminated against on more than 1 of the 9 grounds. This is acceptable.

For example, you may be alleging that you were discriminated against on the grounds of gender, marital status and family status. You simply tick each box beside each of these grounds printed in Part 3 of the Form relevant to you.

However, if you tick these 3 grounds, this does not mean that you now have 3 separate discrimination claims. Instead, it means that you have **1 discrimination claim** based on 3 grounds of discrimination. This is important as your compensation, if successful, will be limited to 1 claim and you will not be treated as if you have 3 separate claims.

Part 4 of the EE1 Form requests you to give a description

of the Claim. This section gives you a number of options to choose from:

(a) Discriminatory Treatment.

This is where you are treated less favourably on 1 of the 9 prohibited grounds but you are still in the employment of your employer or otherwise do not have a dismissal claim.

(b) Discriminatory Dismissal.

This is where you have been dismissed by your employer and you are alleging that this dismissal is discrimination against you on one of the nine grounds.

(c) Harassment.

This is a form of statutory bullying based on you falling within one of the nine protected grounds.

(d) Sexual Harassment.

This is a form of statutory bullying or pestering but with a sexual motivation.

(e) Victimisation.

This is where you have been penalised or punished as a consequence of pursuing a discrimination claim against your employer.

(f) Victimisatory Dismissal.

This is the same as (e) above but the penalisation or punishment has taken the form of a dismissal.

(g) Failure to Provide Reasonable Accommodation.

This is a specific form of discrimination based on the disability ground of protection against discrimination. An employer *is entitled* to refuse to employ, promote or keep in employment someone who is not capable of doing a particular job for which they are required.

    I.   However, an employer *is not entitled* to reach the conclusion that an employee is not capable of performing a job *until* he or she has considered formally what *special treatment or facilities* may be needed to allow the employee to perform the job.

    II.   An employer can refuse to afford the employee those special treatment or facilities only where they impose a disproportionate burden on the business. He must also obtain all relevant and necessary medical information about the illness or disability of the employee. Illness is both mental and physical and includes ailments like alcoholism and drug addiction, depression, stress, eating disorders, whiplash as well as more traditional forms of physical disability.

    III. This disproportionate burden can take the form of financial expenditure and/or disruption to the business and can change from employer to employer depending on the size and resources available to an employer.

    IV. This assessment must be undertaken at all stages of the employment process from recruitment to promotion to retirement. This is known as "reasonable accommodation".

    V.   If you are not provided with this entitlement, you have been discriminated against on the grounds of disability.

(h) Equal Pay.

This is the most established form of equality

protection and essentially ensures equal pay for
equal work or work of equal value. While this
was traditionally based on the ground of gender,
it now applies to all grounds of protection.

(i) A Claim in relation to a Collective
Agreement.
This simply relates to any of the above types of
claim but where the offending breach of the law
is contained in a collective agreement between
an employer and a trade union.

Also, unlike Part 3 of the Form, some of the headings in Part
4 can result in separate compensation awards.

*For example, if you claim, that you have been subject
to discriminatory treatment, discriminatory dismissal and
victimisation, if you are successful, **you will be awarded
compensation under each of these three headings** by the
Equality Tribunal or the Labour Court (on appeal from the
Equality Tribunal).*

On the other hand, if you bring a claim for discrimination,
harassment and sexual harassment, you will be limited to **1
compensation award for all 3 only**. This is dealt with in
this Chapter later. As such, it is important to make sure that
you are properly advised and tick all relevant possible claims
when you fill in the Form otherwise you risk losing possible
compensation claims and being found to be out of time if you
try to make a new Claim later.

Part 5 of the EE1 Form requests details of your legal
representatives. You may have decided to engage a solicitor
prior to filling out this Form. If so, the Solicitor, on your
instructions, will normally fill out the form and ask you to
confirm that you are happy with the details set out.

The Solicitor, in turn, prior to completing the Form may
recommend that a barrister be briefed.

The reason for this is that employment equality claims

**are becoming quite specialised and a precise type of
claim.**

Therefore, it is better to have expertise involved from
the very start so as to ensure that nothing is left out or
overlooked.

Moreover, increasingly, employees will have to make a
choice about where they want to bring their claim.

*For example, if you have been dismissed, should you
bring your claim to the Employment Appeals Tribunal
or the Equality Tribunal? What are the advantages and
disadvantages of both?*

A barrister, specialised in the area of employment law,
can be of great assistance in ensuring that you make the right
decision and can maximise your claim(s). There are a number
of reasons why you would choose to bring your claim to the
Equality Tribunal rather than the Rights Commissioner or
Employment Appeals Tribunal. Some of these are:

(a) **The compensation criteria are broader.** As
we saw in Chapter 1, compensation for an unfair
dismissal before the Rights Commissioner or
Employment Appeals Tribunal is limited to
financial loss attributable to the dismissal.
However, the compensation available to the
Equality Tribunal or Labour Court (on appeal)
or Circuit Court or High Court (on appeal) is
for the "effects of the discrimination".

   I.   While this is also limited to 104 weeks'
        gross remuneration per claim like the
        EAT/Rights Commissioner, there is a
        greater flexibility in how it is awarded
        and can include financial loss as well as
        other headings such as *upset and distress*
        caused by the discriminatory acts.

   II. These are not covered in the Rights

Commissioner/EAT dismissal compensation awards.

III. Therefore, if, as an employee, you calculate that your losses may be small because, for example, you have gotten a new job quite quickly, it may be worth your while taking a discriminatory dismissal claim rather than an unfair dismissal claim as you may obtain a higher amount of compensation based on the upset and distress caused to you *as well as* your financial loss.

IV. Your claim must be related to one of the nine protected grounds however.

(b) The level of proof can be easier to satisfy for an employee before the Equality Tribunal and you do not need 52 weeks' continuous service with your employer;

(c) The Revenue Commissioner treatment of equality compensation can be preferable. The Finance Act 2004 treats compensation for distress caused by discrimination as not subject to tax;

(d) The treatment of injury and illness is better. Unlike the Unfair Dismissal Act 1977-2001, where there is no obligation on an employer to make efforts to provide lighter work for an employee before dismissing on the grounds of incapacity, an employer under the equality route must show they sought to reasonably accommodate an employee.

I. "Lighter work" means work that is less likely to cause further illness or injury exacerbate existing injury or illness.

II. Medical evidence is normally required to show that an employee is medically fit to

return to lighter, lesser or more flexible
duties but not to his previous role in the
workplace prior to illness or injury.

III. On the other hand, if an employee is for
reasons of ill health is unable to return to
work and the ill health is unconnected to
the dismissal, then he is not entitled to
recover compensation under the UDA
1977-2001. This is not the case under the
Equality legislation.

**As such, before you fill in the EE1 Form, you may wish
to engage a solicitor and barrister who can advise you on
all these issues.**

Part 6 of the EE1 Form requests you to fill out details of
the employer. In all official legal documents, the employer is
referred to as the "Respondent".

Request For Information

Part 7 of the EE1 Form relates to a formal **Request for
Information** that you can make to your employer prior to
commencing your claim. There is a specific document that
you send to your employer asking him or her:

(a) Whether he or she agrees with your version of
events,
(b) for an explanation of his or her treatment of
you; and
(c) whether he or she believes that this treatment
amounts to unlawful discrimination.

**This Request for Information document is called the EE2
and is available also on the Equality Tribunal website.**

You can send this to the employer prior to commencing

your claim in order to see if there is an innocent explanation for what happened to you.

The employer replies to this request for information on a specific document called the EE3 Form.

On many occasions, employees are unhappy with the response they get from the employer and proceed with their claims in any event. However, it is an important device because if an employer is misleading in his replies or does not reply at all, this makes the employer appear as if they have something to hide and can be used against him or her at the hearing.

Details of the Complaint Needed

Part 8 of the EE1 Form seeks details of the Complaint itself. This is broken down into the following headings:

(a) Date of First Occurrence of Discrimination.
(b) Date of Dismissal (if applicable).
(c) Date of Most Recent Occurrence of Discriminatory Acts.
(d) Places Where Discriminatory Acts Occurred.

You are then asked to write a brief outline, in your own words, of what happened to you. You will flesh out this outline later in the Written Submissions that you will have to prepare.

Before The Hearing

When you fill out the above details of the Claim Form and this is then referred to the Tribunal, it will initially go to the Equality Tribunal's Secretariat, whose staff will acknowledge your complaint promptly in writing. At this point, you, as the employee, will be referred to in all correspondence from the Equality Tribunal as the "Complainant" and your employer will be referred to as the "Respondent".

Mediation

In this letter back to you or your solicitor, your claim will also now be given a **Case Reference Number**.

If it is an employment equality case, your case reference number will commence with the letters "EE" followed by the year in which the claim was commenced. Therefore, if you commenced your claim in 2009, your claim reference number would begin as "EE/2009".

Very importantly, this letter, confirming receipt of your claim, will suggest that you try **Mediation** to resolve the dispute.

You must be very careful to note that this letter will give you **approximately three weeks to object to mediation**. If you do not object to mediation, it will be assumed that you want to go to mediation and your case will be processed accordingly. If you do object to mediation, your claim will proceed in the normal way to a full hearing.

However, mediation is a very useful, productive way of resolving a dispute if both sides have some remaining element of trust and confidence in each other.

(a) It is very informal and less stressful than a full hearing.

(b) It can be used for any sort of equality claim including dismissals.

(c) The mediator seeks to reach common ground between the parties in terms of any financial settlement or other resolution of the claim.

(d) You can also get a hearing with a mediator far more quickly than a full hearing before an Equality Officer. At the moment, it takes approximately one year or even longer to get a full hearing date before the Equality Tribunal. You can get a hearing before a mediator in approximately three to four months.

Any agreement reached through an equality mediation is fully legally binding on both parties and enforceable by the Circuit Court in the event that either party wishes to break it.

(e) If you do not manage to reach a settlement through mediation, your claim goes back into the system for a full hearing before an Equality Officer of the Equality Tribunal and you will not be delayed by using mediation. Your case will be put back in the waiting list for a full hearing as if you have not opted to go for mediation in the first place.

Make Sure To Give Enough Information

Prior to sending out this first letter to you confirming receipt of the claim, the Equality Tribunal Secretariat will also carry out basic checks to make sure that your complaint appears to be covered by the legislation.

These Are Called "Admissibility Tests"

Only basic admissibility tests are carried out at this stage (further issues about admissibility may be raised by the Equality Officer during his investigation: see below). For this reason also, it is important to be careful when filling out your EE1 Document above.

At this stage, if the complaint appears to be inadmissible to the Tribunal staff, they will write to you, as the complainant, asking you to clarify the factual position. After that, if the complaint still appears to be inadmissible, the case is closed. If it appears to be admissible, or if it is still unclear whether the complaint is admissible, then the Secretariat will send a copy of the complaint form to the Respondent.

Frivolous or Vexatious Claims

The Equality Tribunal has a power to dismiss at any stage proceedings which the Director considers to be brought in bad faith or that are frivolous, vexatious, misconceived or relating to a trivial matter. This decision to dismiss the claim for any of these reasons may be appealed from the Equality Tribunal to the Labour Court within 42 days of the date of the decision.

The Tribunal has a very busy workload and there may be a delay before a case can be assigned for investigation. If this is the case, then the Secretariat will write out to inform the parties of same.

When Does Your Employer Find Out You Are Suing Him?

You do not send your complaint form to the employer. The employer will receive a copy of your complaint form from the Tribunal's Secretariat, as soon as any initial queries about admissibility have been satisfied. (If the Secretariat considers the complaint to be clearly inadmissible, then it may close the case without forwarding it to the Respondent). You do not have to send your complaint form to the employer yourself.

All relevant material received from you, as the complainant, will be copied to the employer so that both parties are fully aware of all the material received by the Tribunal.

Appearance by the Employer

If the employer considers that the initial claims made by the complainant are untrue, inaccurate, that it has a valid defence or that the complaint is not covered by the legislation, it may wish to reply in writing at this preliminary stage, placing these objections before the Tribunal. (However, it *extremely* unlikely that such representation will conclude matters or close the case at that stage).

Investigation of the Complaint: The Next Step

Once the case overcomes the basic admissibility criteria and the respondent has been formally furnished with the complaint by *the Secretariat*, this stage commences when *an Equality Officer* (EO) writes to the parties to inform them that s/he has now been assigned to deal with the case. He will also explain to both parties how he intends to progress the investigation.

There are 2 procedures open to him: the short one and the long one. The latter involves more detailed legal issues. The long procedure is most likely to be the procedure to which the vast majority of claimants are subject.

Long Procedure: Written Submissions

Under this approach, before fixing a date for the hearing, the Equality Officer will conduct an investigation of the complaint. As a first step in that investigation, he will require written submissions from both parties.

Your submissions, as the complainant, are a detailed written account of the complaint:

(a) Setting out the facts and arguments which leads you to believe that you have been discriminated against unlawfully.

(b) The Equality Officer ("EO") should receive the submission (original and 2 copies) within 6 calendar weeks of requesting it.

When the EO receives the complainant's submissions, he will send a copy to the employer, asking him for his or her *replying* submissions within 6 calendar weeks. This replying submission should set out the facts and arguments which convince the respondent that they have not discriminated against the complainant. Again, it is important that the Respondent reply (original and 2 copies) promptly and within the 6 weeks.

The EO will then send a copy of the submissions of the employer to you, the Complainant employee. There is no need for you to draft further submissions in reply (this may be done orally at the hearing).

The main difference between the written submissions and the basic initiating claims forms is that Claim Forms will contain only the bare facts of the claim. However, the Submissions will contain the arguments as to why those facts amount to, for example, unlawful discrimination, dismissal or victimisation. Those arguments can be based on both legal and factual grounds.

In general, your written submissions do not need to follow any set format and do not have to have complicated, legal phraseology. However, they should give a clear, comprehensive and concise statement of fact including:

- What Happened.
- When it Did Happen.
- Who Was Involved.
- Why The Complainant Thinks It Is Unlawful Conduct.
- The Legal Arguments For This Belief.

On a practical level, it is also advisable that you use headings, paragraph numbers and page numbers as this will greatly facilitate reference to extracts of the submissions in the course of the proceedings.

Furthermore, while there is no limitation on the volume or length of the submissions, it is advisable to keep the submissions as succinct and accessible as possible in order to avoid your important points being lost in otherwise irrelevant or less important facts or details.

Copies of all back-up documentation referred to in the submissions, or on which the submissions rely, should be attached to the submissions as an Appendix. This means that each individual document is simply entitled "Appendix A, B, C etc or 1,2,3 etc".

The types of back-up documentation upon which submissions rely may relate to:

- Correspondence between the parties; and
- any internal policy documents or memoranda relevant to the case.

The types of correspondence which can be referred to may also relate to periods of time both before and after the actual *act of discrimination* complained of but before the preparation of the *written submissions*. In other words, open (letters not headed "without prejudice") correspondence from either side or their legal representatives relating to the alleged discriminatory acts can be attached to the submissions where relevant.

The Investigation and Hearing of the Complaint: What Happens Before and On the Day

Investigation (Between the Written Submissions and Hearing Date)

Under the Employment Equality Act 1998-2004, the EO's duty is to *investigate* and decide complaints referred to the Tribunal.

This is different from the role of a civil court or the Employment Appeals Tribunal which decide only on the evidence brought before them and do not conduct any investigation of its own.

If a question arises from the material submitted to the Tribunal (as above), the EO may prior to the hearing date may make additional enquiries in the interests of trying to establish what has happened. These enquiries may be directed to either you or to both you and the (former) employer, or even to third parties, depending on the material available.

For example, the EO may consider it appropriate to direct the employer to produce particular records to see whether they confirm or disprove an inference of discrimination arising from other evidence but which has not been sought already by an unrepresented party. Moreover, the EOs have the following powers when conducting the investigation at this stage:

(a) **Power to enter premises, obtain information and inspect work.**

An EO has powers to obtain information which s/he may require in order to carry out his functions. These powers may be exercised at his discretion. They include the power to:

- Enter premises. If necessary, an EO can even enter a premises by force, on foot of a search warrant issued by the District Court.
- Require any person to produce any records, books, documents etc which are believed to contain relevant information.
- Inspect and copy records.
- Inspect any work in progress at any premises.

An EO may also require any person believed to possess relevant information to attend at the hearing in order to provide information and to answer questions (see below).

(b) **Non-Compliance With the Investigation.**

Where an EO is of the opinion that any person has failed to comply with the requirement to produce or provide access to any material information, he may apply to the Circuit Court seeking an order compelling the person to comply with the requirement.

(c) **Obstruction of the EO.**

It is an offence to obstruct or impede an Equality Officer in the exercise of his powers or to fail to comply with a requirement of an EO.

The penalties provided by the Act are:

- On summary conviction, a fine of up to €1,905 or imprisonment for up to 1 year or both.
- On conviction on indictment, a fine of up to €31,743 or imprisonment for up to 2 years or both.
- Where the offence continues after conviction, a further fine of up to €317 per day on summary conviction and up to €1,905 per day on conviction on indictment.

Preliminary Matters

As a matter of practice, procedural issues often arise prior to the actual substantive hearing itself.

If you are bringing **an equal pay claim,** as well as written submissions, preliminary hearings will automatically be arranged by the Equality Tribunal. In particular, the Tribunal will arrange work inspections and identify issues such as who your comparator is and what he or she does, job classification schemes and pay scales. Also, the Tribunal will want to identify the main legal issues required to be heard at the substantive hearing.

In other types of claim, the Director of the Equality Tribunal may direct the holding of preliminary hearings to resolve other preliminary issues also. In general, a preliminary hearing may be held into any question that arises relating to the entitlement of any party to bring or defend proceedings. In particular, a number of particular issues into which a preliminary hearing may now be held include:

- Whether the complainant has complied with the requirements relating to referrals such as time limits.
- whether the complainant is an "employee". or
- any other question relating to law or fact.

Therefore, if there are admissibility tests that were raised by the employer when you started your case, instead of stopping your case at the very beginning, the EO can now hear those arguments at this stage.

Hearing

After all of this process is complete, when the Equality Officer finally considers that the case is ready, the Tribunal will contact the parties to arrange a hearing of the complaint as soon as practicable. Reasonable notice will be given (normally about 6 weeks). The hearing is not too formal or intimidating and is held in a modern office type environment.

The EO actively directs the hearing. At the outset, he will explain the format to the parties.

It is an inquisitorial style hearing. This means that it is different to the EAT style hearing set out in Chapter 1. The investigation depends less on the parties questioning each other themselves but on the EO questioning both sides him or herself.

The EO will ask questions of each party himself directly, even if they have representatives with them. Moreover, normally, time is not spent formally reading out the documentation that you or your lawyers have submitted to the Tribunal (as above), such as the written submissions. Needless to say this documentation can be referred to or quoted by the parties, if required.

After he has finished asking questions of you as the employee and the employer, the EO will also ask relevant questions that arise of any witnesses you and your employer bring along with you on the day. The nature of these questions changes from case to case, the aim is to see if both sides can prove their different version of events.

In employment equality cases, the burden of proof lies with the complainant who, in the submissions, evidence and the answers he gives, has to show that a *prima facie* case of discrimination exists.

This simply means that the evidence you give the EO in both your story and your supporting documentation must be enough to show him or her that there is an arguable case that you were discriminated against by your employer.

If you can do this, the pressure is now put on the employer who, in order to successfully defend their case, must, now in their answers and evidence, show that what is alleged did not occur at all or, if it did occur, that they were driven by factors that were non-discriminatory.

In order to show you have an arguable case, you must satisfy the following 3-fold test:

- That you are covered by one of the relevant nine grounds in the Act,
- that you have been subjected, as a matter of fact, to the treatment complained of, and
- that this treatment is less favourable than the way someone who differs from you on that ground is, was or would be treated in similar circumstances.

However, in practice, the hearing does not formally run along this 2-step line in terms of *its procedures*.

The EO simply questions both parties (as above) generally to adduce the evidence from them and only applies this burden of proof test *afterwards* in the written decision. In other words, there is not a formal point at the hearing when the EO will

announce that the burden has now shifted to the employer/
respondent and then direct his questions accordingly.

**The EO will not decide at the hearing whether the
claimant has made out an arguable (in Latin *"prima
facie"*) case, and then turn to the respondent for him to
discharge his burden.**

The parties will not know whether they have done enough
to win or defeat a case until the written decision arrives. (For
example, an employer will not know until the written decision
that he has defeated a case.)

As a result, as the employee, you have to make sure that
the get the maximum amount of evidence out in your answers
to the EO's questions at the hearing in order to boost your
position and undermine the other side's positions.

This "inquisitorial process" means that the EO effectively
does an examination and cross-examination of the parties
himself for a substantial part of the hearing.

Examinations and cross-examinations were explained in
Chapter 1 dealing with the EAT/Rights Commissioners.

Once the EO has asked all the questions he considers
necessary and relevant, only then do the representatives of
the parties, if you have engaged lawyers, get the opportunity
to examine and cross-examine.

The EO will give each party directly (or through their
representatives) the opportunity to make any points they wish,
to ask witnesses (including the employer/respondent and his
witnesses) their own questions and to comment on the points
made by the other.

Essentially, the purpose of the questioning of the other
side is to catch them out or undermine their story. It is this
role (as well as making any particular legal points that may
arise) rather than presenting the factual evidence *per se* in
which solicitors and counsel are particularly useful. At this
stage, the complainant goes first, then his witnesses. This is
followed by the Respondent and his witnesses.

However, the hearing is not taken on oath.

Each party may call witnesses to give evidence on their behalf. The witnesses may be allowed to remain throughout the hearing, or may be allowed to come in only to give their own evidence. Parties may also ask the EO to allow other persons to be present for a range of reasons, e.g., to take notes or provide moral and emotional support ('support persons').

The Equality Tribunal has a further power to order any person to attend before the Director or at a hearing, and to provide (bring with them) information which is considered relevant. This is in effect like a *subpoena* that the EAT can use and is set out in Chapter 1. No such order will be made unless the requesting party applies in a reasonable time to allow the person (the subject matter of the order) sufficient notice to attend a hearing. This application must be made before the hearing date. You must also provide sufficient information to satisfy the Tribunal that the person requested does in fact have relevant information in order to exercise its functions and that it is necessary for it to direct their attendance.

An employment equality hearing normally last between ½ day to a full day (from 2 to 4 hours).

At the end, the EO will normally allow the representatives of each side to sum the entirety of the evidence they have given and to make submissions on the other side's evidence (in other words, to undermine it).

When this is done, the EO will end the hearing and reserve his decision.

Expenses

The Equality Officer has the power to award expenses of one party against another party considered to have obstructed or impeded the investigation. However, such expenses may **not** include the costs or expenses of legal representatives. Like the unfair dismissal route, you do not get your legal costs, if you are successful, before the Equality Tribunal. However, if you bring an equality claim relating to gender to the Circuit

Court and you are successful, you do get your legal costs paid
by the other side.

Remedies

Where a decision is in favour of a complainant, the range of
redress options you can get is one or more, as appropriate,
of the following:

- Arrears of equal pay (up to a maximum amount
  of 3 years' loss of salary prior to the date of
  you started your claim. This loss is calculated
  as the difference between what you were paid
  and what you should have been paid had you
  been paid equally).
- Prospective equal pay from date of referral
  onwards.
- Compensation "for the effects of the
  discrimination or victimisation" occurring
  not more than 6 years prior to the date of the
  referral.
  - The maximum amount of compensation
    for any one claim is fixed at a maximum
    of 104 weeks' gross remuneration
    where the claimant is in employment **or**
    €12,700 for a person who was not in the
    employment of the employer when the
    discrimination occurred (for example, if
    you were refused employment after a job
    interview, you will be limited to the lesser
    compensation figure). Equal Pay claims
    have a different compensation system as
    set out above and are not subject to the
    104 weeks' remuneration ceiling.
  - However, where the conduct complained
    of comprises of discrimination *on more*

than 1 of the 9 discriminatory grounds, the statutory ceiling is nonetheless limited as if it was one claim comprising of just one discriminatory ground (in other words, 104 weeks' remuneration only).

- Similarly, if a cause of action comprises of discrimination on more than 1 of the discriminatory grounds *as well as* harassment or sexual harassment, it is similarly limited to 1 maximum ceiling of 104 weeks' remuneration only.

• An order for equal treatment in any relevant respect. This means that the person you successfully sued will be ordered to change their ways going forward.

• An order that a specified person take a specified course of action.

• An order for reinstatement or reengagement with or without compensation.

Interest may be awarded on any financial amounts ordered to be paid but only in gender cases.

Settlements and Pre-Hearing Consultations

In the area of equality claims, how settlements and your consultations with your lawyers work are very much the same as in unfair dismissal claims. As such, Chapter 1 of this book deals with Employment Settlements and Consultations. However, the way in which compensation is awarded in employment equality cases is different and may be more generous. This has now been set out above in this Chapter. As such, you must bear in mind these differences in compensation when thinking about the type of financial compensation or other redress you may be willing to accept in a settlement.

If You Are Not Happy With The Equality Determination?

If this is the case, you will have to appeal the determination of the Equality Officer within 6 weeks of the date of the determination to the Labour Court.

The Labour Court Appeal

The Labour Court process is more formal than the Equality Tribunal process and is more like a traditional court in that it is not inquisitorial but more adversarial. You must prepare written submissions and comply with the directions of the Labour Court Secretariat in a way similar to that set out in this Chapter for the Equality Tribunal. Full specific details of the Labour Court procedure are set out at www.labourcourt.ie.

Because of the similarity in the pre-hearing procedures, many claimants use the same Written Submissions for the Labour Court as they used for the Equality Tribunal. If you are preparing new Submissions, you must be very careful that there are no major inconsistencies in the facts and that your case remains substantially the same. The Labour Court appeal is a brand new hearing of your case. However, if you change your story significantly, you risk being found to lack credibility and being found unsuccessful.

Therefore, the following guidelines are important in terms of preparing the substance of the submissions for you as the employee in the Labour Court. Your employer will also be using the same style in his or her submissions in reply to you.

(a) They should commence by being addressed to the Labour Court.
(b) In the case of both the claimant and respondent respectively, each set of Written Submissions should state the full background to the case

in as comprehensive and detailed a manner possible. In other words, the claimant sets out the background to the case as he sees it in his submissions. It is important to make sure that the locations, dates and identities of individuals to be adduced in evidence be confirmed and recorded accurately in the submissions.

(c) Each set of written submissions should then summarise the nature of the dispute and as each side sees it. This should include a summary of:

    i.   How the dispute arose; and

    ii. the position of the party in relation to the dispute.

(d) Although it is not desirable to include extensive legal submissions in the Submissions, it is nonetheless advisable that each party raise any legal points upon which they propose to rely and any legal grounds and caselaw for same. In this regard, the Written Submissions may be further divided between "Factual Submissions" and "Legal Submissions".

(e) The submissions may then include a statement as to the opinion of the party as to how the matter should be resolved.

Again, these Written Submissions must have been given to the Labour Court Secretariat on Haddington Road, Dublin 4, well in advance of the hearing in compliance with the time scales set out to you or your lawyers in letters you will have received from the Labour Court. These Submissions must also have attached to them all records, photographs, documents that you wish to show the Labour Court. 6 copies of these Written Submissions must be provided to the Labour Court.

What To Appeal

You must also be careful in deciding what to appeal.

You do not have to appeal the whole of the EO's determination.

> *For example, you may be happy with some of the determination but not with other parts. Suppose you brought a discrimination claim and a dismissal claim before the Equality Tribunal and you only win on the discrimination claim. If you appeal the whole determination, you risk losing before the Labour Court even those parts of the EO's determination with which you are happy. If you have been completely unsuccessful before the EO, then you will probably wish to appeal the whole decision. However, if you have been partially successful, you will not wish to appeal that aspect of the determination.*

As such, in the Appeal Form to the Labour Court available at www.labourcourt.ie, you must specifically identify those parts of the Determination of the EO that you wish to appeal.

Cross-Appeals

If you appeal the determination of the EO, it is most likely that the employer will also appeal any aspect of the determination he or she may wish to overturn, if any.

As such, suppose you have succeeded in your discrimination claim and not in your dismissal claim, if you appeal the dismissal finding, your employer is likely to appeal the discrimination finding also.

This is known as a "Cross-Appeal".

One way that some employees and their legal advisers try to avoid this from happening is to leave it until the very last minute to lodge the appeal in the hope that the employer will not have enough time to enter an appeal of his or her own against you. This is because the employer also only has six weeks from the date of the determination to appeal and may be out of time to bring his or her own appeal by the time he learns of your "last-minute" appeal.

Therefore, you must carefully consider, if the determination was not as good as you hoped, whether you are willing to gamble away and open up the whole determination before the Labour Court.

Moreover, like the Equality Tribunal, you will not be awarded your legal costs before the Labour Court if you are successful.

Therefore, if you have engaged lawyers to represent you, you must ask yourself whether the extra expense in legal costs will be justified by the compensation or other redress you hope to obtain from the Labour Court?

If you have been completely unsuccessful in front of the Equality Officer, you may take a view either that you have nothing to lose and appeal or to simply give up before you spend even more money with little prospect of a return. Again, this is a matter upon which your legal advisers will be able to give you advice.

Location of Labour Court

In the Greater Dublin Area

Whilst the Equality Tribunal predominantly sits in Dublin only, the Labour Court sits in Dublin and around the country. The Equality Tribunal Offices are located on Clonmel Street, off Harcourt Street, Dublin 2. Also, like the Employment Appeals Tribunal, the Equality Tribunal and Labour Court have their own designated hearing rooms in the Dublin area. These are at the Labour Relations Commission, Haddington Road, Dublin 4.

Outside of the Greater Dublin Area

Outside of the Dublin, Labour Court hearings are held in hotels. Labour Court judges are extremely specialised and well trained for their role. Unlike the Employment Appeals Tribunal whose Chairperson tends to be also a practising solicitor or barrister, the Labour Court Chairperson is a permanent and full-time professional adjudicator of employment law matters.

The Judges of the Labour Court

Like the Employment Appeals Tribunal, the Labour Court hearing will have a panel of 3 judges. One will be from a trade union background, one from an employer background and a Chairperson. However, the 3 judges at all times will be very courteous to all parties in the dispute irrespective of whether they are the employer or employee side.

The Labour Court Hearing

The Labour Court hearing will be formal but the judges (known as "panel member") will be very conscious of the fact that you will be nervous. The Hearing Room is laid out with a top table for the 3 judges and 2 other tables facing each other in front of the judges where you sit at one table and the employer sits at the other table. There will also be a person called the "Registrar" sitting in the room.

The Procedure of the Hearing is very like that of the Employment Appeals Tribunal set out already in Chapter 1 in that the judges will introduce themselves at the start of the hearing and there will be examination and cross-examination of all witnesses including questions from the judges themselves to the parties in the course of the hearing.

However, there are some differences.

Length of Hearing

Normally, the Labour Court lists its hearings **for 1 full day** rather than "half a day". One full day is about 5 hours in length. This means that there is a greater chance that you will finish your case in one day and not have to incur further legal costs returning for a second day.

If necessary, the Labour Court will arrange a second hearing date for the case if it does not finish on the first day. It normally will take about 2 months to get a second hearing date after the end of the first hearing depending on the availability of everyone involved to have the second hearing day.

Opening of Hearing

The opening of the Labour Court hearing is also different to the start of an Employment Appeal Tribunal hearing. At the start, you or your legal adviser will stand up (unless excused by the judges from doing so) and read out the Written Submissions you have prepared to the Court. Depending on the length of the Submissions, this can take some time.

When your Written Submissions have been read out, the employer or his legal representatives will then read out their Written Submissions. These will normally deny what you claim against them and set out their version of what happened. The Submissions will also contain legal points that can be complicated to understand but which your lawyers and the court will deal with. Normally, the Labour Court will not expect you to be able to deal with legal points and will address your lawyers directly on those points.

After reading out the Submissions, both parties will have a brief opportunity to reply to each other's submissions.

Questioning of Witnesses

Once the Written Submissions are dealt with, the judges move into the hearing and the examination and cross examination of witnesses begins. In the course of the Labour Court appeal, if you, as the employee have appealed, you will be known as the "Appellant" and the employer will be known as the "Respondent". If the employer has appealed, you will be known as the "Respondent" and he or she will be known as the "Appellant".

Redress before the Labour Court

The Redress and compensation available to the Labour Court in an Employment Equality Appeal is exactly the same as that set out earlier for the Equality Tribunal. You will normally get a written determination from the Labour Court within 8 to 10 weeks of the final hearing date. If you are unhappy with the Labour Court judgment, there is only one appeal to the High Court but on a point of law only. In other words, you cannot reopen the whole case again but only where there is some law or piece of legislation that you say that the Labour Court incorrectly applied or ignored and you want this clarified as it might affect the outcome of your case. However, if you take this appeal to the High Court, you will be liable for the full legal costs of your own legal team and that of the employer in the event that you are unsuccessful.

CHAPTER 3

The Civil Courts

Grounds for Going To Court

Clearly, the civil courts remain an important forum for the resolution of employment disputes. For employment disputes, the most important Civil Courts are:

(a) The Circuit Court.
(b) The High Court.
(c) The Supreme Court.

This is what you probably think of when you see the word "court". These are the courts where the judges and barristers wear wigs and are held in old wood panelled rooms. These courts are the formal, traditional places where legal disputes are heard. They are subject to strict, precise and formal time scales and legal documentation. It is also common for employees to have both a barrister and a solicitor for these cases. Again, the reason for this is that a barrister is an expert in court procedure and presentation.

The Circuit Court

If you have an employment dispute, you will find yourself in the Circuit Court where:

(a) There is an appeal of a determination of the Employment Appeals Tribunal. This appeal may be brought by the employee or the employer. It is heard in the Circuit Court under the Unfair Dismissals Acts.

I. The Circuit in which the appeal should be brought is the Circuit in which the employer (not the employee) ordinarily resides or carries on the profession, trade or business.

II. In this situation, the Circuit Court can overturn an earlier favourable decision for the employee and award legal costs against the losing side. This is unlike the Employment Appeals Tribunal itself which cannot award legal costs to the winning side.

III. Determinations of the Employment Appeals Tribunal are enforceable in the Circuit Court. This is different to an appeal. It means that there has been no appeal of the determination and the employer also has not complied with the EAT determination.

IV. Therefore, in the event that you have a determination in your favour that the employer is not complying with, you can bring proceedings before the Circuit Court to obtain a Court Order forcing the employer to comply.

V. The Circuit Court can also order an employer to pay you interest on the compensation that he owes you. There are specific procedures and court documents that must be used in order to bring an appeal to the Circuit Court and it must be brought within 6 weeks of the date that the determination of the EAT was communicated to the parties.

VI. The type of redress available from the Circuit Court is the same as in the

Rights Commissioner Service and the Employment Appeals Tribunal.

(b) You can have your employment dispute heard in a Circuit Court if you are taking a gender discrimination case under the Employment Equality Act 1998-2004. This means that, if your case is gender related, you can decide to go straight to the Circuit Court instead of the Equality Tribunal. This has previously been discussed in Chapter 2. This has a number of advantages.

    I.   In the event that you are successful before the Circuit Court, you will be awarded your legal costs as well as any compensation for the effects of the discrimination or breach of the equal pay rules.

    II.   It is also likely that you will have your case heard more quickly before the Circuit Court than the Equality Tribunal.

    III. A further major benefit of the Circuit Court jurisdiction in the equality area is that there is no limit on the amount of money that the Circuit Court can award you and it is not limited to its more general compensation ceiling of €38,000.

    IV. If you have gone to mediation and entered into a mediated settlement before the Equality Tribunal mediation service which an employer is not complying with, then you can enforce this mediated settlement in proceedings before the Circuit Court.

(c) You can have your employment dispute heard before the Circuit Court if you chose to challenge the employer on the basis that he has breached a contract he has with you. This contract is your contract of employment. Unlike an unfair dismissal, where the entitlements of an employee are set out in the legislation, a breach of contract claim depends on the interpretation of the judge of the terms of the employment contract and not the unfair dismissals legislation. This type of claim is called a "Wrongful Dismissal".

Difference Between An Unfair/Discriminatory and Wrongful Dismissal

The biggest consequence of this difference between an unfair/equality and wrongful dismissal is that the compensation available under the unfair dismissals and the employment equality rules (set out in Chapters 1 and 2 of this book respectively) do not apply to a wrongful dismissal claim.

Under wrongful dismissal, the courts do not award damages for the period of time you spent unemployed seeking new employment or compensation for the effects of discrimination or victimisation against you.

Damages Limited to Your Notice Period

Instead, if you are successful in your claim that your contract of employment was breached, you will most likely be awarded damages (compensation) limited to **the notice period to which you were entitled prior to your contract being terminated**.

If you have been paid for or worked out your notice period, then you have no claim for wrongful dismissal as the courts consider that you have suffered no unlawful, economic loss and will not entertain the claim unless you can show some other type of economic loss for which you are entitled to damages.

For example, suppose you are an employee and a shareholder of a company and the board of directors are purporting to terminate your employment and unlawfully forfeit your shareholding in the company. Depending on the contracts involved, even if you have no loss for your termination of employment, you are still entitled to your shareholding or damages for the forfeiture thereof. But this is a shareholder issue is separate contractual claim and is not related to your status as an employee directly.

The reason for this approach is that wrongful dismissal claims do not protect fairness of the decision or of the procedures used by the employer in selecting you for dismissal. In short, the traditional approach of the courts in Ireland was that no one was entitled to a job for life and so long as your employer gave you reasonable notice then you could be dismissed at will. This is the major rule in wrongful dismissal cases.

What was a reasonable period of notice depends on what is written into your contract or, if your contract is silent, the type of job you do and your professional status.

For example, for a dismissed professional employee, reasonable notice might be up to six months notice. As a result, if you were not given this reasonable notice prior to dismissal, you were entitled to financial damages for this lack of reasonable notice as redress.

If the amount of compensation you believe or are advised you might be awarded for your wrongful dismissal exceeds €38,000, then you must bring the case to the High Court instead of the Circuit Court. The High Court would apply the same principles applicable to the Circuit Court for wrongful dismissal cases as set out above.

The High Court and Injunctions

Wrongful dismissals cases have the particular advantage that **an injunction** can be awarded against an employer restraining him or her from acting in a certain way, such as terminating your contract, until the full trial of the action.

An injunction is simply a legal device ordered by a court against a party to prevent them from doing something that they would otherwise do in its absence.

A breach of an injunction order is a very serious offence and is a contempt of court which can result in large fines and/or imprisonment. There are 3 types of injunction:

(1) **Interim Injunction.**

This is the quickest and most short term form of protection. Normally, the court only hears one side of the story before awarding this injunction to stop someone doing something as the matter may be so urgent that there may not be enough time to inform the other side (the person being stopped or injuncted) and arrange their attendance in court. This person is only informed of the injunction immediately after the court order is made against them. It is the easiest type of injunction to get and normally lasts as a temporary "holding device" until the court hearing for an interlocutory injunction. You only get the interim injunction if the matter is extremely urgent. Otherwise, you bypass the interim stage and apply instead for an interlocutory injunction.

(2) **Interlocutory Injunction**

This is a more formal application where time

> allows for both sides to be now informed of
> the application and are in attendance in court.
> Normally, evidence of what is happening is
> presented to the court in a document called
> an "Affidavit".

What Is An Affidavit?

This is a written document setting out the various versions
of events of the employer and employee and sworn under
oath by the person telling their story in front of a witness.
This injunction, if awarded, is not the end of the case. It will
normally only last for a few months and is only designed to
maintain the *status quo* (prevent change) pending the full trial
of the dispute before the court. An interlocutory injunction
will normally require the employer not to dismiss an employee
and to continue their salary and benefits pending the full trial
of the action.

> (c) **Perpetual Injunction**
> This is a rare injunction and may be awarded
> as part of the decision of the full trial of the
> case preventing the employer from doing
> something going forward into the future. It
> may be of an indefinite duration rather than
> pending any further trial.

**You cannot bring a case just to get an injunction in itself.
An injunction is normally brought as part of some other
type of court proceedings.**
    The most common is a wrongful dismissal claim.

Advantages Of An Injunction

Therefore, the ability to obtain an injunction as part of a
wrongful dismissal case has a very important advantage

over the EAT, Rights Commissioner or Equality Tribunal which cannot restrain a dismissal but only offer redress *after it has happened*. Moreover, while these bodies can order re-instatement and re-engagement, the longer you are out of the workplace, the less likely it is that you will be returned to work there.

Therefore, because it takes a number of months to get a hearing date before these bodies and then a further number of months before a determination is made and then the possibility of further appeals, an employee may see the chances of being restored to his job become slimmer and slimmer as time goes by.

As such, an injunction is very useful in preventing the damage being done to your employment in the first place.

Also, an injunction, if awarded, is a very useful tool in encouraging an employer to settle a case as now he or she is saddled with the prospect of keeping you on their payroll for an extended period of time in circumstances where the court has found that their actions are potentially unlawful.

However, injunctions and wrongful dismissal claims are very risky and not to be entered into lightly. There have been many cases where the injunction application has gone on for a very long time. Moreover, if you seek an injunction and are unsuccessful, you are now left with the prospect of being exposed to additional and very high legal costs for yourself and the employer before the main trial even occurs. Remember, getting an injunction does not win the case in itself. It simply restrains the employer from doing something pending the full trial of the case.

The Supreme Court

This is the highest court in Ireland and only hears cases in this area on appeal from the High Court. Here the parties undertake the risk of very high legal costs and long delay in having their dispute resolved.

Civil Court Procedure

The way a case is presented before a civil court such as the Circuit or High Court is very similar to that already set out in Chapter 1 of this Book relating to the Employment Appeals Tribunal. However, it is normally more formal and more legalistic. The major difference is that there will only be one judge hearing the case. Moreover, if you are in the High Court or Supreme Court, it is normal that your legal team will now comprise the following:

(a) Solicitor.
(b) Junior Counsel (Barrister).
(c) Senior Counsel (Barrister).

While it is not compulsory to have a senior counsel, the reason that you will engage a senior counsel for the High Court is due to the following:

(a) The higher financial risks to which you are now exposed in terms of legal costs.
(b) The very high level of expertise and experience required for running a High Court action where complex and detailed issues of law may be disputed.
(c) The preparation and presentation of court documents and the extra weight and credibility behind attempts at out of court financial settlements.

In the High Court or Supreme Court, in the event that you are successful or settle your case, the fees of your legal team, including senior counsel, will be covered. On the other hand, if you lose your case, the fees of every single lawyer involved in the case, including those of your employer, will be paid for by you. This can result in an immense bill and must be factored into any decision to bring your case to the High Court.

It is not as common to have senior counsel in the Circuit Court. In this court, junior counsel run the vast majority of cases. The term "junior counsel" is a formal title reflecting the fact that a barrister has not yet "taken silk", namely, become a senior counsel. Many "junior" counsel are extremely experienced and this title is not to be taken as meaning that they are not experienced or experts in their area. Moreover, the scale and level of legal fees are not as high in the Circuit Court and the costs risk is therefore less.

As such, on the day of the hearing, whether in the Circuit or High Court, there will be:

> (a) Opening Submissions.
> (b) Examination, Cross-Examination and Re-Examination of all witnesses, including the "Plaintiff" (employee), by the barristers for both sides. This means that the witnesses will be asked questions by the barristers for both sides about their evidence in the case.
> (c) Questions posed to the witnesses and to the barristers by the judge.
> (d) Closing submissions.

This will all be done in the formal setting of a court room. As such, you must be sure that your case will stand up to the very detailed scrutiny to which it will be subjected in questioning by the lawyers and the judge. A Circuit Court case normally finishes within 1 day in a matter of hours. On the other hand, a High Court action can run into a number of days depending on the complexity of the issues and the number of witnesses called.

One major difference between the civil courts and bodies like the EAT is that the civil courts can make orders that increase the information you have about a case before the trial. Two important applications you can make to the court against your employer is:

(a) An Application for an Order of Discovery.
(b) An Application for Replies to Particulars.
(c) An Application for Interrogatories.

In effect, an Order for Discovery relates to the documents relating to your case that are in the power, procurement or possession of your employer. The big benefit to this order is that the employer must give you the documents within a strict time scale and well before the hearing of the case.

The other two applications relate not to documents but to pieces of information and specific details you can ask the employer relating to the employer and to the case.

CHAPTER 4

Industrial Relations

What Are My Options Here?

This is another route an employee with a grievance can use. This concerns the existence of "a trade dispute" under the Industrial Relations Acts 1946-2004.

Trade Dispute

The term "trade dispute" is so wide as to encompass almost any dispute between an employee or former employee and the employer. When there is a "trade dispute" is judged subjectively. This means that so long as the employee honestly believes there is a dispute, then the court cannot refuse to hear his case on the basis that there is not a trade dispute.

There are 2 ways in which a trade dispute could be tackled by an employee.

The first relates to an employee pursuing a grievance through a picket of the workplace.

Option One: Industrial Picketing

What the employer has to fear from this legislation is that so long as the employees go through certain steps they could eventually take industrial action in the form of strikes, pickets, a go slow and that action would not unlawful.

Part II of the Industrial Relations Act 1990 contains the main body of the law on industrial action. Generally, provided certain conditions are met, employees cannot be sued for engaging in industrial action which could include peaceful picketing. In other words, employers cannot go to High Court to injunct a picket.

If an employee wanted to bring a dispute to the point of industrial action the following steps would be needed:

1. Join a registered trade union.
2. Avail of procedures agreed by custom and practice or in collective agreements, e.g. grievance procedure.
3. Ensure it is a trade dispute, in particular that it connected with employment or non-employment of a worker.
4. Carry out a secret ballot in accordance with union rules and the legislation.
5. Union gets sanction from ICTU.
6. Give notice of one week to employer that will engage in secret ballot.
7. Engage in peaceful picketing.

Therefore if an employer wants to avoid such action they should insert in the contracts of employment that any grievance should first be brought under the workplace grievance procedures before any industrial action is threatened, then try and settle the matter at that stage.

Option Two: Industrial Relations Proceedings

This is the second procedure where the employee pursues his claim through the Rights Commissioner and/or Labour Court. This is a useful procedure where an employee can refer a "trade dispute" to a Rights Commissioner or in some cases to the Labour Court.

Why Use This Route?

Where an employee is dismissed but has less than 1 year's service and does not have a discrimination claim, they often claim under this procedure to a Rights Commissioner (or on appeal to the Labour Court).

This is also a useful procedure where an employee is still in employment and may not want to provoke a resignation situation.

As such, one can bring an Industrial Relations (IR) dispute before the Rights Commissioner (RC) and get an adjudication on something that it is too risky to run before the courts such as:

- Bullying at work.
- Non-application of company procedure.
- Change in terms of employment such as work hours or location.
- Dismissal.

The only problem is that while an IR recommendation is "binding" in the IR sense, this is not a legal avenue of redress. In other words, if an employer appears before a RC, he "agrees to be bound" by the determination of the RC. However, if he reneges on this and refuses to comply with the RC's determination, the only relief for an employee is a threat of picketing. However, where there is no trade union in the workplace (as is the case with up to 70% of Irish employers), the threat is diminished significantly.

Moreover, if the employer refuses to appear before the RC at all (in the absence of a unionised workplace), then the case must go at first instance to the Labour Court. If the employer also refuses to appear before the Labour Court, there is little an employee can do to compel attendance.

An employer may refuse to appear as, under the IR Acts 1946-1990, (as with the RC) there is also no method of legally enforcing a Labour Court determination against an employer.

This is not to be confused with the role of the Rights Commissioner and Labour Court under the unfair dismissals and equality routes respectively discussed in Chapters 1 and 2 of this book which are enforceable.

The IR legislation does not apply to public sector employers that are "manifestations of the State".

Industrial Action 2001-2004

New Industrial Relations legislation from 2001 and 2004 now creates a new procedure where an employer who does not enter into a collective bargaining situation with employees and the internal grievance procedures have not resolved a problem. An employer can now be compelled by the Labour Court to grant such terms and conditions of employment as determined by that Court.

CHAPTER 5

General Employee Rights

In this Chapter, we look at rights available to employees in the event of disputes in the workplace. In particular, we look at the procedures leading up to dismissal. We also consider the all important and sometimes difficult area of leave entitlements.

It is important to remember that the courts and tribunals that we have looked at already in this book deal with many of the disputes relating to the rights set out in the Chapter. As such, if you want to know what to expect when putting your case together, you can simply refer to Chapters 1 and 2 of this book.

PART A: FAIR PROCEDURES

It is important that you now check the Disciplinary Policy and Procedure in your workplace, so you know the procedures that apply to you in the event that your employer is unhappy with some aspect of your performance or conduct. This is an important factor in deciding whether you have been unlawfully dismissed.

Warning!
There is no specific procedure that an employer must follow.

However, all employers have to ensure that their employees are fully aware of what they are doing wrong and are given an opportunity to improve. If your employer does not have a policy and procedure for disciplinary and grievance issues at work, it means that he or she is seriously in breach of your legal entitlements. In practice, there are 2 types of workplace problems that disciplinary procedures deal with.

These are:

(a) Less Serious Problems.
(b) More Serious Problems.

Less Serious Problems

Warning!
Normally, a warning process is used for less serious problems in the workplace such as absenteeism or poor performance. Other offences such as aggression, theft or bullying are considered more serious and are known as gross misconduct.

Therefore, the basic minimum that an employer should do for dealing with less serious offences is the following:

* The employee must first be given a **Verbal Warning** (May be recorded on the file for a specific period of time),
* then comes a **First Written Warning** (Placed on a file for a definite period time), and
* at last, there is a **Final Written Warning** (Warning that the next step is dismissal).

If the employee's performance is poor, these warnings should be accompanied with some enquiry as to the reason for the problems and some form of offer of training or assistance in the workplace to improve the performance of the worker. If the employee has not changed his behaviour or performance after this process is finished, then the next step is dismissal.

More Serious Problems

What Is This?

If the employee is accused of something out of the ordinary that is very serious, then he is accused of gross misconduct and may be dismissed without his notice. However, the employer must first have a full investigation. This is different to the court and tribunal hearings set out in the previous chapters of this Book.

Here, we deal with an investigation into allegations internal to the workplace itself. The workplace is not a courtroom and therefore the procedures are not as detailed.

However, there are certain basic legal entitlements that exist in relation to how these internal investigations in the workplace must be handled. Again, you must check your workplace policy and procedure in order to be sure of the specifics that apply to you.

However, a*t the very least*, an employee is entitled to be:

- Informed of the charge against him or her.
- Given an opportunity to answer it.
- Given an opportunity to make submissions.

The Charge

Three Important Tips!

(1) The employer must not only furnish the employee with any documents relating to what he or she is accused of, but with all the other information upon which the employer is relying or may rely in arriving at a decision about him or her.

(2) An employer or investigator must not act on the basis of information that he has not

> disclosed and furnished to the employees
> involved in the investigation. This is the
> case even if the consequence of the decision
> may not ultimately be dismissal but rather
> damage to the reputation and good name of
> an employee.
>
> (3) The person ultimately investigating a
> complaint or charge against an employee must
> have no part in the events or situations relating
> to the allegations against an employee.

Answering the Charge and Making Submissions

Two Types
An employee may answer a charge and make submissions
by meeting with his employer on a one–to-one basis ("an
inquisitorial approach").

He may wish to have a hearing with both parties present,
and an opportunity either himself or through a representative
to test by cross-examination the evidence of the complainant
against him.

Representation of the Accused Employee

In any interview or investigative hearing of a charge (and
any disciplinary hearing), an employee is entitled to be
represented. If the matter is so serious that the employee
may be dismissed, then normally a legal representative such
as a solicitor is entitled to be present. However, normally,
the solicitor is there simply to observe the meeting and is not
supposed to interrupt or participate unless something very
improper is occurring.

The right to be represented must be made known to the
employee at the time such a hearing or meeting is proposed.

Also, an employee is not entitled, automatically, to

cross-examine a person making accusations against them or their witnesses. Whether this is appropriate will depend on the particular circumstances of the charge. 3 important circumstances determine whether an oral hearing should be granted:

(a) The seriousness of the allegation against the employee or the importance of his rights in issue as they relate to his continuing tenure of employment, his good name and to his livelihood.

(b) The extent to which there is a dispute of the facts between the parties.

(c) Is the complainant in a position to give evidence? A complainant who has been subject to serious bullying may already be in a vulnerable and fragile state mentally and emotionally. Therefore, it may not be appropriate to allow his or her bully or a representative to confront the complainant in the adversarial context of a cross-examination at an oral hearing. This may, in fact, exacerbate the situation. In such a case, the employer may be justified in refusing to allow a confrontation to occur.

PART B: MATERNITY LEAVE

Basic Maternity Leave

Women who commence maternity leave on after March 1, 2007 will be entitled to 26 weeks' basic leave and 16 weeks' unpaid additional leave. An employee must start her maternity leave now at least 2 weeks prior to the expected date of confinement.

Additional Maternity Leave

This is a separate period of leave and is unpaid to which an employee is entitled in addition to her basic maternity leave. She is entitled to take an additional period of 8 weeks commencing immediately after her basic maternity leave

Hospitalisation and Illness of the Baby

An employee may now ask her employer to postpone a period of her maternity leave during the period of hospitalisation of a newborn that becomes ill. An employer may agree to this at his or her discretion. If the employer agrees, the employee may return to work and then use the balance of the outstanding leave period when the baby comes out of hospital. In order to avail of this facility, an employee must have taken at least 14 weeks of her maternity leave by the time the postponement is required and 4 of these weeks must have been after the child was born. When leave is postponed and the employee returns to work, then the employee may take the resumed leave in one bloc starting not later than 7 days after the baby is discharged from hospital.

Ante-Natal Care Classes

An employee is entitled to paid time off to attend 1 set of ante-natal care classes but not the last 3 of the classes as the employee would have commenced maternity leave by that stage. The expectant father is also entitled to paid time off work to attend the last 2 ante-natal classes.

Breastfeeding Rights

If the employee is breastfeeding and the baby is less than 6 months old, she will be entitled to some paid time off each day to breastfeed. An employee may avail of this entitlement is either of 2 ways.

She is entitled to time off work (without loss of pay) for the purposes of breastfeeding in the workplace where facilities for breastfeeding are provided *in the workplace* by her employer. An employer is not obliged to provide such facilities where their provision would amount to a cost, other than a nominal cost, to the employer.

She is entitled to a reduction in her working hours (without loss of pay) for the purpose of breastfeeding otherwise than in the workplace.

As such, women who are in employment and are breastfeeding are entitled to take one hour (with pay) off work each day as a breastfeeding break until the baby is 6 months old. This may be taken as:

> (a) 1 60-minute break, or
> (b) 2 30-minute breaks, or
> (c) 3 20-minute breaks.

Return To Work

An employer is obliged to allow the employer to return on the (duly notified) expiry of her protective leave. Since October 18, 2004, this means she is entitled to return:

> (a) With the same employer with whom she was working immediately before the start of her period of leave, or if ownership of her employer has changed during her leave, with the new employer.
> (b) In the same job she held immediately before she commenced her leave.
> (c) Under the same contract of employment under which the employee was employed immediately before the start of that period

(hours, pay rates etc) or, if a new owner has taken over, under an identical contract with that new owner. In either case, this means a contract that is not less favourable and that incorporates any improvement to the terms and conditions of employment to which the employee would have been entitled had she not been so absent from work.

Suitable Alternative Employment

In the event that they cannot return employees to the same job on their return from protective leave, an employer must nonetheless return employees to a suitable alternative job.

PART C: ADOPTIVE LEAVE

Adopting mothers or sole male adopters who commence adoptive leave on or after March 1, 2007 are entitled to 24 weeks' Adoptive Leave attracting a payment. They are also entitled to 16 weeks' unpaid additional leave. The payments are payable by the Department of Social and Family Affairs.

PART D: CARER'S LEAVE

Entitlement To Carer's Leave

If you have been employed for a period of at least 12 months' continuous employment by your employer, you shall be entitled to leave for the purposes of providing full time care and attention. This leave period cannot not exceed 65 weeks.

It applies when:

(a) The person to whom the employee proposes to provide full-time care and attention is a "relevant person". A relevant person is a person who has a disability that requires full time care and attention and who:
   • Has attained the age of 18 years; or
   • is under the age of 18 years and is a person of whom an allowance is paid for domiciliary care of "handicapped" children under section 61 of the Health Act 1970.

(b) The employee provides the employer with a decision from the Department for Social, Community and Family Affairs by a deciding officer that the person in respect of whom the employee proposes to avail of carer's leave in order to provide full time care and attention is a relevant person.

(c) During the period of leave, the employee provides full-time care and attention to the relevant person.

(d) During the period of carer's leave, the employee does not engage in employment or self-employment.

Warning!
All the above conditions must be satisfied before the employee is entitled to undertake carer's leave.

PART E: ANNUAL HOLIDAY LEAVE

What Am I Owed?

In calculating how many days' paid holidays an employee may be entitled to, an employer must include:

- All hours worked.
- Time spent on previous periods of annual leave.
- Time spent on maternity leave.
- Parental leave periods.
- *Force majeure leave* periods.
- Adoptive leave periods.
- Time spent on the first 13 weeks of Carer's leave.

What Am I Not Entitled To?

Employees do not accrue annual leave entitlements for:

- Sick leave
- Occupational injury.
- Temporary lay-off.
- Career break.

How Is It Calculated?

An employee shall be paid annual leave equal to:

(a) 4 working weeks in a leave year in which he or she works at least 1365 hours;
(b) One third of a working week for each month in the leave year in which he or she works at least 117 hours;
(c) 8% of the hours she or he works in a leave year (subject to the maximum entitlement of 4 working weeks).

If more than one of the above methods is available, the employee is entitled to the one which provides him with the most generous annual leave.

When Can I Take It?

The employer has discretion as to when annual leave may be taken having regard to work requirements. However, the employer must take into account:

> • The need for the employee to reconcile work and family responsibilities, and
> • the opportunities of rest and recreation of the employee.

An employer must consult with the employee and/or his trade union in this regard.

The holidays must be given to an employee within the leave year to which the hours worked relate. However, with the consent of the employee, all or a portion of annual leave may be taken within 6 months of the commencement of the following leave year.

It is the duty of the employer to ensure that their employees take all their leave entitlements within the appropriate period.

Public Holidays

Public holidays are defined in the Second Schedule of the Organisation of Working Time Act 1997 and are:

> (a) Christmas Day.
> (b) St Stephen's Day.
> (c) St Patrick's Day.
> (d) Easter Monday.
> (e) First Monday in May.
> (f) First Monday in June.
> (g) First Monday in August.
> (h) Last Monday in October.
> (i) New Year's Day.

Overall, there are 9 public holidays in any leave year and employees, with the exception of part-time employees, have an immediate entitlement to public holiday benefits.

PART F: PARENTAL LEAVE

What Is It and How Is It Calculated?

This applies to everyone who is the natural or adoptive parent of a child.

Parental leave can be taken in the form of days off or hours off during the day. However, it should equate to:

> • The hours worked in an agreed 14 week period before the parental leave period. For example, if you work a set or agreed 20 hours per week. The leave is 20 x 14. This is 280 hours parental leave entitlement; or
> • where your hours per week are subject to change, then you get *14 times* the average number of hours per week. The average is calculated from the weeks that the employee worked in the 14 week period ending immediately before commencement of the week in which leave is taken.

Where an employee is entitled to parental leave in respect of more than one child, the total leave cannot exceed 14 weeks in any period of 12 months without the employer's consent.

Annual leave must be taken at such other time as determined by the employer when it falls within a period of parental leave.

In relation to public holidays, where an entitlement arises during a period of parental leave, a day is added to the period of parental leave in respect of each public holiday.

Notice Provisions

A minimum of 6 weeks' notice in writing of intention to take parental leave must be given to the employer specifying:

- The date of commencement,
- the duration of leave, and
- the manner in which it is proposed to be taken.

The notice must be signed by the employee.

Confirmation Document

At least 4 weeks before taking the leave, the employer and the employee must then sign **a confirmation document**.

The employer and the employee are obliged to retain the confirmation document.

Once this is signed, your leave cannot be interfered with by the employer.

Proving Parenthood

In relation to establishing proof of parenthood, if the child is adopted the employer is entitled to call for evidence of the dates of birth of the child and the making of the adoption order. In respect of any other child, the employer can call for "evidence in relation…to the employee being a parent of the child and the date of birth of the child".

The employer is only entitled to evidence as may be "reasonably" required.

Postponement, Curtailment and Variation of Leave By The Parties

Once a confirmation document has been signed, the employee

is not entitled to work during the agreed period of parental leave. Also, the employer cannot force you to postpone or cancel once you sign this document.

Be Aware!

However, the *parties may agree* to postpone, curtail or vary the leave at any time. Curtailed or postponed leave may be taken at another time by agreement with your employer.

Postponement By Employer

Prior to the signing of the Confirmation Document, employers may decide to postpone parental leave entitlement. However, they can postpone for no more than 6 months. This must be done by notice in writing (to be retained by the parties) at least 4 weeks prior to when it was thought leave would commence.

They can only do this where the taking of parental leave would have a substantial adverse effect on the business, occupation or profession by reason of:

(a) Seasonal variations in the volume of work concerned,

(b) the unavailability of a person to carry out the duties of the employee in the employment,

(c) the nature of those duties,

(d) the number of employees in employment,

(e) the number of employees in the workplace whose periods, or part of whose periods, of parental leave will fall within the period specified by the employee in their notice, or

(f) "any other relevant matters".

Be Aware!

No confirmation document must have been signed by the parties if the employer wishes to force a postponement.

An employer may not postpone the commencement of leave more than once in relation to a particular child unless the ground for postponement is seasonal variations in the volume of work, in which case, the commencement of leave may be postponed twice.

Index